W9-ANR-577

LENT AND EASTER
PRAYER AT HOME

LENT AND EASTER
PRAYER AT HOME

MARK G. BOYER

ave maria press   Notre Dame, Indiana

All biblical quotations are taken from the *Contemporary English Version*, copyright © 1995, American Bible Society, 1865 Broadway, New York, NY 10023. Used with permission. All rights reserved.

© 2002 by Ave Maria Press, Inc.

All rights reserved. No part of this book may be used or reproduced in any manner whatsoever, except in the case of reprints in the context of reviews, without written permission from Ave Maria Press, Inc., P.O. Box 428, Notre Dame, IN 46556.

www.avemariapress.com

International Standard Book Number: 0-87793-971-3

Cover and text design by Katherine Robinson Coleman

Cover and interior photos by Photodisc

Printed and bound in the United States of America.

Library of Congress Cataloging-in-Publication Data
Boyer, Mark G.

Lent and Easter prayer at home / Mark G. Boyer.
     p. cm.
ISBN 0-87793-971-3 (pbk.)
1. Lent--Prayer-books and devotions--English. 2. Holy Week--Prayer-books and devotions--English. 3. Eastertide--Prayer-books and devotions--English. 4. Catholic Church--Prayer-books and devotions--English. I. Title.
BX2170.L4 B694 2002
242'.3--dc21
                                   2001005602
                                          CIP

Dedicated to my great nephew,

Zachary David Ingram,

and my great niece,

Rebecah Jane McElyea

Peter said to Cornelius and his household:

"Jesus was put to death on a cross.

But three days later, God raised him to life and let him be seen.

Not everyone saw him.

He was seen only by us, who ate and drank with him after he was raised from death.

We were the ones God chose to tell others about him."

Acts 10:39-41

Contents

INTRODUCTION

Lent and Easter Prayer at Home is designed as a guide for daily prayer using the familiar signs and symbols that surround us during the seasons of Lent and Easter. It can be easily used by families, small groups, and individuals who wish to deepen their appreciation of these rich seasons.

Lent and Easter Prayer at Home is divided into three sections: Lent, Holy Week, and Easter. There are fifty-nine entries, each consisting of six parts: Title, Scripture, Reflection, Meditation, Prayer, and Memories. The Title focuses on a sign or symbol in our homes or churches. The Scripture is taken from either the Old or New Testament and highlights the place of these signs and symbols in our faith tradition. The Reflection aims to stimulate our thoughts and helps us make a connection between God and the celebration of Lent, Holy Week, and Easter. The Meditation encourages personal contemplation or journaling to chronicle our spiritual growth. The Prayer, a few verses from a psalm, summarizes the ideas presented in the Scripture, the Reflection, and the Meditation.

The section titled Memories contains suggestions for personal record-keeping. This section offers ideas for recording your stories about the people and things of Lent, Holy Week, and Easter in your home. As you record these memories, perhaps in a special bound blank book just for that purpose, keep in mind that you are recording some of your family's most precious history.

Beginning on page 117, you will find "Blessings for Lent and Easter." These short family prayers bless all that is part of your home during these seasons. They can be used and adapted as you see fit.

It is my hope that, through the use of this book, you will be awakened to God's presence through the signs and symbols of Lent, Holy Week, and Easter—this year and for many years to come.

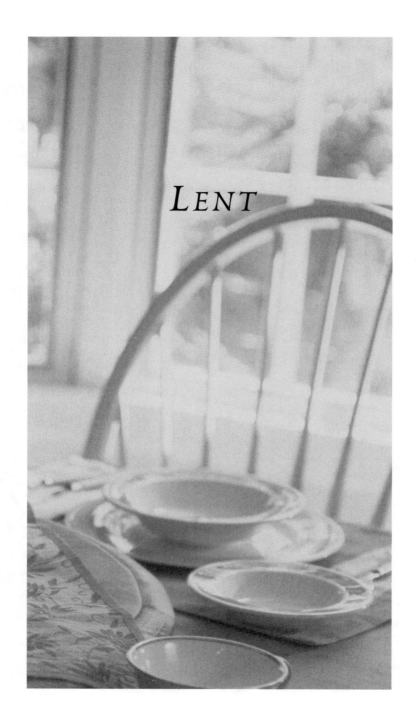

LENT

Mardi Gras

Eating and drinking make you feel happy . . .
(Ecclesiastes 10:19).

Reflection:

The literal meaning of Mardi Gras is "Fat Tuesday."
Mardi Gras is the day before Ash Wednesday, the
beginning of Lent. Traditionally, it is the last day of
merry-making before the discipline of fasting, almsgiving,
and prayer of Lent begin. It is sometimes called Shrove
Tuesday to point toward the penance or sacrifice in which
a person will engage throughout the forty days of Lent.

In the ancient world, Mardi Gras was not about the
partying that goes on in New Orleans and Rio de Janeiro
today. It was the last day to eat of the fat that was left over
from the previous fall's meat supply. The fasting of Lent
required that people not eat any meat as well as other
specific food products like milk, butter, and cheese.

In our health-conscious culture, it might not be a bad
idea to fast from some meat during Lent. Certainly, one
does not want to put his or her health at risk, but then a
few days without meat might force us to look at other
foods, such as vegetables and fruits and fish, that might
make us healthier.

Meditation:

How can you observe Mardi Gras and eliminate
some of the fat in your diet?

Your love is faithful, LORD. You give your guests a feast in your house, and you serve a tasty drink that flows like a river. The life-giving fountain belongs to you, and your light gives light to each of us (Psalm 36:5, 8-9).

M e m o r i e s :

What types of Mardi Gras celebrations have you observed in the past?

Carnival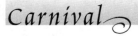

S c r i p t u r e :

The LORD said to Moses, "I have heard my people complain. Now tell them that each evening they will have meat and each morning they will have more than enough bread. Then they will know that I am the LORD their God" (Exodus 16:11-12).

R e f l e c t i o n :

When most of us hear the word "carnival," we think of games and prizes, rides and sideshows, and all types of food. Most of us are not aware that the word means "farewell to flesh." In the ancient world, the period of feasting and revelry before Lent was carnival time, an opportunity to enjoy the last of the meat slaughtered and preserved from the previous fall. Once Lent began, no meat was supposed to be consumed.

It may not be a bad idea to consider eating up the meat we have around before Lent begins this year. Why? Because doctors tell us that we eat too much meat, especially red meat, and a diet rich in fruits, vegetables, and grains is better for us. Thus, carnival time could be a great occasion to begin to make some changes in our freezers, refrigerators, pantries and, thus, in our diets.

Any type of change in our routine will be taxing, especially if it means that we will have to change menus and pay closer attention to what we are buying at the grocery store. Any change we make in our lives, if it is to remain in place, will require concentration and discipline. One approach might be to consider this Lent as a time to make some changes in your lifestyle and save the carnival for the fifty days of Easter.

Meditation:

What changes do you need to make in your diet and lifestyle to make you a better person? What steps do you need to take to make these changes?

Prayer:

In heaven I have only you, and on this earth you are all I want. My body and mind may fail, but you are my strength and my choice forever. Powerful LORD God, it is good for me to be near you (Psalm 73:25-28).

Memories:

What changes have you made in your diet in the past? If they stayed in place, what did you do? If they didn't stay in place, what have you learned from your previous attempts?

Lent

Scripture:

On the last and most important day of the festival, Jesus stood up and shouted, "If you are thirsty, come to me and drink! Have faith in me, and you will have life-giving water flowing from deep inside you, just as the Scriptures say" (John 7:37-38).

Reflection:

The Old English word "Lent," meaning "the lengthening of days," refers to spring when winter's short days are transformed into summer's lengthening hours of daylight. Gradually, it came to describe the time of fasting and penitence between Ash Wednesday and Easter, consisting of forty weekdays. Because all Sundays are considered to be "little Easters," during Lent they are not considered appropriate for acts of penance.

Unlike today, when you simply go to the grocery store when your pantry gets low or empty, larders used to be mostly empty by spring. What had been gathered and stored in the fall was just about exhausted. So, most fasting was not freely embraced; it was a condition of life.

For the discipline of Lent to have any affect on our lives, it has to be freely embraced. In our society where so many are overweight, we fast in order to limit our intake of food. We pursue Lent's other two disciplines, almsgiving and prayers, with a similar mindset. We give alms in order to feed those who have fasting imposed on them. And we intensify our prayer to listen more intently to the God who wells up within us, like life-giving water.

Meditation:

What do fasting, almsgiving, and prayer mean to you?

Prayer:

Our Lord, you bless everyone that you instruct and teach by using your Law. You give them rest from their troubles. Justice and fairness will go hand in hand, and all who do right will follow along (Psalm 94:12-13, 15).

Memories:

What disciplinary practices are you engaging in this Lent? Make a list, and for each indicate what change you hope the practice will make in your life.

Ashes

Scripture:

When the king of Nineveh heard what was happening, he also dressed in sackcloth; he left the royal palace and sat in dust (Jonah 3:6).

Reflection:

Dust or ashes can be found everywhere, beginning with the coffee table in your living room. The wood-burning fireplace or stove, the campfire, burned leaves, the trash barrel, a forest fire, a burned down house, a fraternity or sorority bonfire—all leave dust and ashes behind. Even the calcium left after a cremation is referred to as human ashes.

On Ash Wednesday, approximately forty days before Easter, we take a few moments to have ashes traced on our foreheads in the sign of the cross. Those ashes are the residue of last Passion (Palm) Sunday's green fronds, which, once dried, were burned.

Ashes remind us not to take this life too seriously. All persons, all things, pass away—even us. On Ash Wednesday we are, literally, brought face to face with our future—ashes—and given the opportunity to repent and to reform our lives—like the king of Nineveh when he heard the prophet Jonah.

Meditation:

How is your life like ashes? How much of it has already turned into ashes? What repenting or reforming do you need to do?

Prayer:

I pray to you, LORD! Please listen. Instead of food, I have ashes to eat and tears to drink. My life fades like a shadow at the end of day and withers like grass (Psalm 102:1, 9, 11).

Memories:

Put a bowl of ashes in a prominent place, such as on the table where you eat your meals. Use the Blessing of Ashes in the back of this book.

Ask each member of your family to share his or her memory of an Ash Wednesday. Keep a record of these stories.

Almsgiving

SCRIPTURE:

When you give to the poor, don't let anyone know about it (Matthew 6:3).

REFLECTION:

One of the traditional Lenten practices is almsgiving, the art of giving away treasure, time, and talent in the hope of setting a pattern in ourselves for the rest of our lives. While almsgiving may directly concern the poor, it has a broader application, too.

We give away our treasure to help others. We might consider food, clothing, or money as treasure to be shared. Time can be given to help in a local soup kitchen, rehabilitation center, or learning center. Mentoring a young man or woman is another way of sharing our treasure of time. Giving away talent means using our gifts for others, like helping prepare taxes, cooking, sewing, using computer skills, or teaching.

The Lenten practice of almsgiving reminds us of how interdependent we are. And when we practice almsgiving, we discover something else—that what we give away we get back over and over again.

What treasure, time, and talent are you giving away this Lent?

Prayer:

I treasure your word above all else; it keeps me from sinning against you. I praise you, LORD! Teach me your laws (Psalm 119:11-12).

Memories:

What time, talent, or treasure have you given away in the past that came back to you?

Fasting

Scripture:

Jesus said: "When you go without eating, don't try to look gloomy as those show-offs do when they go without eating. I can assure you that they already have their reward. Instead, comb your hair and wash your face" (Matthew 6:16-17).

Reflection:

Before a blood test or surgery, we are told to fast from food, usually from midnight. Fasting leaves us empty and in need, and that is why it is a good practice during Lent.

But the purpose of fasting is not just to deny ourselves food. The emptiness following fasting should put us in contact with those who are in need and, then, move us to share some of what we have with them. Emptiness also makes us aware of our need for God—the only one who can fill us.

In a consumer-oriented, fast-food culture like ours, we find it difficult to fast. Someone is always offering us something to eat. No kitchen cabinet is without its supply of snacks. No refrigerator is without its leftovers. As a self-imposed discipline, fasting helps us to control our desire for immediate self-gratification. It reminds us that we are on a journey, one which food cannot adequately and eternally satisfy.

While fasting is voluntary, the church sets a minimum standard during Lent. According to Canon Law, anyone who is eighteen years old is obligated to fast on Ash Wednesday and Good Friday. The church defines fasting as eating one full meal a day with the provision that the other two meals do not equal the full one in quantity.

Meditation:

Besides food, from what else can you fast? How will your fasting raise your awareness of your dependence on God?

Prayer:

I will celebrate and be joyful because you, LORD, have saved me. Liars accuse me of crimes I know nothing about. When they were sick, I wore sackcloth and went without food. I truly prayed for them (Psalm 35:9, 11, 13).

Recall a self-imposed fast of the past. What did your fast teach you about yourself, others, and God?

Abstinence

Scripture:

The LORD said: It isn't too late. You can still return to me with all your heart. Start crying and mourning! Go without eating (Joel 2:12).

Reflection:

Abstinence refers to the Lenten practice of voluntarily not engaging in an appetite or craving. During Lent, many people abstain from smoking, alcohol, sex, or certain foods, like candy, ice cream, or meat. The purpose of abstaining from some of life's pleasures is not for the sake of endurance, but for the sake of imposing discipline on one's life.

Voluntary abstinence is practiced in order to foster our growth, to curb our appetites, to raise our awareness concerning all we enjoy and how often we indulge in those activities. Abstinence is also embraced so that we can begin to set in place changes in our lifestyle. The purpose is not to endure giving up something for forty days only to indulge in it once Easter arrives. That does no one any good, because no change or growth results. In this latter scenario, Lenten abstinence becomes a game we play.

While abstinence is voluntary, the church sets a minimum standard during Lent. According to Canon Law, anyone who is fourteen years old is obligated to abstain from eating meat on Ash Wednesday, the Fridays of Lent, and Good Friday.

Meditation:

With what self-discipline does abstinence help you? From what are you abstaining now?

Prayer:

I pray to you, LORD! Help me to guard my words whenever I say something. Don't let me want to do evil or waste my time doing wrong with wicked people. Don't let me even taste the good things they offer (Psalm 141:1, 3-4).

Memories:

How has the practice of abstinence helped you make changes in your life in the past?

Prayer

Scripture:

When you pray, don't be like those show-offs who love to stand up and pray in the meeting places and on the street corners. They do this just to look good. I can assure you that they already have their reward. When you pray, go into a room alone and close the door. Pray to your Father in private. He knows what is done in private, and he will reward you. When you pray, don't talk on and on as people do who don't know God. They think God likes to hear long prayers. Don't be like them. Your Father knows what you need before you ask (Matthew 6:5-8).

Reflection:

Along with abstinence and fasting, prayer is a Lenten practice meant not to increase the quantity of prayers, but the quality of our life of prayer. During times of prayer, the sense of independence that our culture prizes comes face to face with dependency on God, a prime characteristic of a follower of Jesus.

Prayer is our acknowledgment that everything we have is a gift from God. Nothing can be earned or deserved—not even our life. Once we understand that, prayer becomes less of what we say to God and more of what God says to us. Our job is to listen and act on what we have heard.

The requirements for prayer are simple. Alone, we place ourselves in the presence of the omnipresent God. And with open hands and open heart and open mind we trust that God will give us what is best for us, that God will fill us with compassion, that God will lead us to where God wants us, and that whatever words escape from our lips will be put there by God. Often referred to as doing God's will, prayer makes us realize that we are totally dependent upon God.

Meditation:

How does your prayer foster your dependence upon God?

Our God, you deserve praise in Zion, where we keep our promises to you. Everyone will come to you because you answer prayer. Our terrible sins get us down, but you forgive us. You bless your chosen ones, and you invite them to live near you in your temple (Psalm 65:1-4).

Memories:

On a time line, trace the evolution of your prayer life. How has your method of prayer changed over the years?

Penance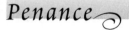

Scripture:

The Law came, so that the full power of sin could be seen. Yet where sin was powerful, God's kindness was even more powerful. Sin ruled by means of death. But God's kindness now rules, and God has accepted us because of Jesus Christ our Lord. This means that we will have eternal life. What should we say? Should we keep on sinning, so that God's wonderful kindness will show up even better? No, we should not! (Romans 5:20–6:2).

Reflection:

Everyone talks about sin, but few ever define it. Those doing the talking presume that those doing the hearing already know what sin is. But instead of presuming that it refers to any thought or deed, any commission or omission, what happens if we begin to think of sin as human failure, the inability to respond to God as fully as possible? After all, that's how Paul thought of sin in his letter to the Romans.

Our inability to fully cooperate with God, according to Paul, has been removed through God's kindness, and Jesus has demonstrated how it can be done. Notice that Paul isn't interested in sins, the result of human failure, but in sin, the human condition that existed before Jesus showed us how to relate to God.

During Lent, then, we examine the degree of our cooperation with God. Whatever we need to change in our life becomes the subject of penance, the self-imposition of an activity or prayer in order to correct or fine-tune our relationship with God. We don't engage in acts of penance in order to atone for our sins or earn salvation, because we can't. Out of infinite kindness God has already done that and welcomed us as coworkers in God's plan of saving the world.

Meditation:

What acts of penance are you imposing on yourself this Lent? How is each designed to foster your cooperation with God?

Prayer:

Our God, you bless everyone whose sins you forgive and wipe away. So I confessed my sins and told them all to you. I said, "I'll tell the LORD each one of my sins." Then you forgave me and took away my guilt (Psalm 32:1, 5).

MEMORIES:

How did you used to understand Lenten penance? How has the change in your understanding altered the way you observe Lent?

Stations of the Cross

SCRIPTURE:

Jesus was taken away, and he carried his cross to a place known as "The Skull." In Aramaic this place is called "Golgotha." There Jesus was nailed to the cross, and on each side of him a man was also nailed to a cross (John 19:16-18).

REFLECTION:

Especially during Lent, many people follow the last few hours of Jesus' life through a devotion known as the Stations of the Cross. Usually numbering fourteen or fifteen, the stations—stopping places along Jesus' journey from Pilate's residence to Golgotha—depict scenes of his suffering, death, burial, and resurrection.

A station offers us a place to stop, to think, to reflect, and to pray. We slow down long enough to stay in one place for a few minutes. With the help of the depiction of the event, we call to mind the occasion of Jesus' suffering, crucifixion, death, or resurrection. Then, through reflection, we make a connection to our lives. What happened to Jesus has happened to us—not in exactly the same way, but similar nevertheless. Our prayer focuses on asking God to help us to cooperate with God's work in all the events of our lives.

While they may not be the official Stations of the Cross, each of us can make a personal list. These might include birth, baptism, confirmation, first eucharist, graduation, marriage, birth of a child, job promotion, death of a grandparent or parent. Through our stations, we begin to see the thread of God's plan tying together our lives, just like we see the string of God's love woven through the events of Jesus' life.

Meditation:

What are your Stations of the Cross? Make a list. Then identify the thread that ties all of them together.

Prayer:

Let my words and my thoughts be pleasing to you, LORD, because you are my mighty rock and my protector (Psalm 19:14).

Memories:

If you have attended a public service of the Stations of the Cross, made them privately, or seen the pope make them in the Colosseum, what is your favorite station? Why?

Cross

SCRIPTURE:

Christ rescued us from the Law's curse, when he became a curse in our place. This is because the Scriptures say that anyone who is nailed to a tree is under a curse (Galatians 3:13).

REFLECTION:

The cross has been so sanitized that it no longer shocks us. Its wood may still bear the body of Jesus, but the warm flesh tones, the carefully painted drops of red blood, the neatly tucked-in white loin cloth, and the gold-trimmed blue I.N.R.I. banner above his head make Roman capital punishment acceptable.

In the ancient world, a cross was a sign of defeat. The person nailed to the wood was thought of as cursed by God. Crucifixion would never have resulted if the individual had not done something displeasing to God. Since Jesus died as a common criminal on a cross, almost no one could think that he was God's anointed one.

What the paradox of the cross teaches us is that victory is achieved exactly where we presume God will not be victorious. The Son of God is not found on a throne, but nailed to two pieces of wood. Jesus is not recognized in life, but in death. God is revealed to be exactly where we wouldn't look.

MEDITATION:

In what experiences of your life have you experienced the paradox of the cross?

The LORD watches over all who honor him and trust his kindness. He protects them from death and starvation. We depend on you, LORD, to help and protect us. You make our hearts glad because we trust you, the only God (Psalm 33:18-21).

MEMORIES:

Do you have a cross or crucifix in your home? If so, identify where you got it and display it during Lent. Use the Blessing of a Cross in the back of this book.

Zion

SCRIPTURE:

Sound the trumpet on Zion, the LORD's sacred hill. Warn everyone to tremble! The judgment day of the LORD is coming soon. The LORD said: "It isn't too late. You can still return to me with all your heart. Start crying and mourning! Go without eating" (Joel 2:1, 12).

REFLECTION:

We begin Lent with ashes and the words of the prophet Joel calling us to conversion from the top of Zion, God's holy mountain of Jerusalem and its Temple with God's inner dwelling place. The purpose of the trumpet blast is to signal the time and the need for all to turn toward God and away from everything that leads them in the opposite direction.

In many ways, conversion has become a buzz word and lost a lot of its fire. Authentic conversion implies a realignment of our lives, change that reaches to the core of who we are, a transformation of attitudes, an alteration of values, a revision of our relationship with God. The traditional Lenten practices of almsgiving, prayer, and fasting can aid us in our authentic conversion endeavor.

Such is what our keeping of Lent is about. Such is what our keeping of Easter attempts to hold into place so that what we began during Lent and what was observed during Easter becomes our new way of living throughout the rest of the year, and maybe even the rest of our lives. Thus, Joel's call to Zion involves a trembling before the presence of God, who, with our cooperation, transfigures us into new people.

Meditation:

What converting do you need to do this Lent?

Prayer:

From east to west, the powerful LORD God has been calling together everyone on earth. God shines brightly from Zion, the most beautiful city. Our God approaches, but not silently; a flaming fire comes first, and a storm surrounds him. God comes to judge his people (Psalm 50:1-4).

What authentic conversion have you undergone in the past? How did you keep those changes in place in your life?

Reconciliation

Scripture:

Even when we were God's enemies, he made peace with us, because his Son died for us. Yet something even greater than friendship is ours. Now that we are at peace with God, we will be saved by his Son's life (Romans 5:10).

Reflection:

Our celebration of the sacrament of Penance is associated with the confessing of our sins to a priest and receiving absolution. But that ritual represents the culmination of all the reconciling in which we have been engaged throughout our lives. That's why we focus on reconciliation during Lent.

A husband tells his wife that he doubted her evaluation of a situation. She forgives him. They are reconciled and grow deeper in love. In a sudden burst of anger during play, one child strikes another. An adult encourages one child to say, "I'm sorry," and the other to say, "I forgive you." Play resumes. Both children are reconciled. Friends, who acknowledge mistakes to each other, restore their relationship and experience reconciliation all the time.

The author of all reconciliation is God. Even when we are not able to make peace with God because of great guilt, God reconciles us to Godself. That's the power of love. That's the effect of reconciliation.

Meditation:

What has been your most recent experience of reconciliation?

Prayer:

With all my heart I praise the LORD, and with all that I am I praise his holy name! With all my heart I praise the LORD! I will never forget how kind he has been. The LORD forgives our sins, heals us when we are sick, and protects us from death. His kindness and love are a crown on our heads (Psalm 103:1-4).

Memories:

What has been your greatest experience of reconciliation? Who was involved? How did your experience draw you closer to God?

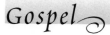

Gospel

Scripture:

This is the good news about Jesus Christ, the Son of God (Mark 1:1).

Reflection:

The Greek word for "gospel," usually translated into English as "good news," literally means, "the good news of the victory." Not originally being a religious word, it was used by the runner sent to the city to announce the good news of the king's victory so that the people could prepare to welcome home their conquering leader.

Only the author of the Gospel according to Mark calls his work a gospel. Matthew calls his a book, Luke calls his a narrative, and John does not give his a name. Biblical editors name as gospels the four accounts of Jesus' ministry. For Mark's Gospel the good news of the victory is not that Jesus has defeated evil, but that God has conquered death through Jesus' dying and rising.

According to Mark, God is present where people presume God not to be—such as in the abandonment Jesus experienced on the cross, the silence of the tomb, and in the life of God's reign. Both Lent and Easter are meant to awaken us to all those experiences of our lives where God is presumed not to be but where God chooses to be. Each of those is good news of God's victory for us.

Meditation:

In which of your experiences, those you at first thought had nothing to do with God, have you discovered the good news of God's victory?

Prayer:

My God, my God, why have you deserted me? Why are you so far away? Won't you listen to my groans and come to my rescue? I cry out day and night, but you don't answer, and I can never rest (Psalm 22:1-2).

What is your personal gospel? Take time to note its major parts and what good news God has entrusted to you.

Incense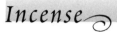

SCRIPTURE:

Another angel, who had a gold container for incense, came and stood at the altar. This one was given a lot of incense to offer with the prayers of God's people on the gold altar in front of the throne. Then the smoke of the incense, together with the prayers of God's people, went up to God from the hand of the angel (Revelation 8:3-4).

REFLECTION:

Incense, a sweet-smelling mixture of gums, resins, and spices, is often burned on charcoal in a censer during Lent and Easter. As the Book of Revelation indicates, the swirling smoke represents our prayers rising up to God. In the days when people thought of the universe as consisting of three stories—God on the top, people in the middle, and the dead on the bottom—burning incense functioned as a good metaphor for prayer.

Incense can still serve as a metaphor for prayer if we focus on its olfactory characteristic. When we are surrounded with incense's smoke, either in church or at home, we are reminded that we are in God. We usually think that we are separate from God, when the fact of the matter is we are always in God's presence—whether we are aware of it or not.

Incense also reminds us that our lives are spent in service to God and others—not understood separately but corporately. Our service of God through prayer leads us to the needs of others, and meeting others' needs sends us back to prayer.

Meditation:

What service of God led you to meet someone's needs? What service to another person led you to God?

Prayer:

I pray to you, LORD! Please listen when I pray and hurry to help me. Think of my prayer as sweet-smelling incense, and think of my lifted hands as an evening sacrifice (Psalm 141:1-2).

Memories:

What church service do you remember because incense was used? How did the sweet smell lead you into God?

Altar

The Lord meant that when you eat this bread and drink from this cup, you tell about his death until he comes (1 Corinthians 11:26).

Reflection:

In almost every church there is an altar. It may be square or rectangular in shape, but it serves as the Lord's table. Being both altar and table indicates that it is where the sacrifice of Jesus on the cross is celebrated and where the meal commemorating his once-for-all offering is eaten. The broken bread is the body of Christ, and the cup is the blood of Christ. But bread is food meant to be eaten, and the cup is drink meant to be drunk. So the altar of sacrifice is also a banquet table around which the friends of Jesus gather to share a meal.

The place around which you gather with your family in your home serves as both an altar and a table. Food that has been sacrificed is placed upon it. Something had to die in order for you to live—the cow had to die to give you hamburger or steak; the potato had to die in order to give you the vegetable; and the grains of wheat had to die in the earth, grow, and die again as they were ground into flour, kneaded, and baked to give you bread. So, around your table/altar you and your family nourish your bodies on that which has been sacrificed for you.

In so doing you proclaim death. Around the Lord's altar/table we remember Jesus' death and wait for his coming in glory, as we feed on his body and blood. Around your family table/altar, you remember that without food you die and that some things must die for you to live. Food and death are intimately connected no matter whose altar/table you gather around.

Meditation:

What other connections do you find between food and death, a table and an altar?

Prayer:

What must I give you, LORD, for being so good to me? I will pour out an offering of wine to you, and I will pray in your name because you have saved me. You are deeply concerned when one of your loyal people faces death (Psalm 116:12-13, 15).

Memories:

What important meals do you remember eating from your table? How did each involve food and death?

Ambo

The one who gives life appeared! We saw it happen, and we are witnesses to what we have seen. Now we are telling you about this eternal life that was with the Father and appeared to us. We are telling you what we have seen and heard, so that you may share in this life with us (1 John 1:2-3).

REFLECTION:

The ambo, the place for the proclamation of the word of God, is often referred to as the pulpit or podium. From it we are served God's word as nourishment for our spirits. When the scriptures are proclaimed, God speaks to us. Particularly in the gospels, it is Jesus who proclaims himself to us. He is the eternal Word, spoken by God since the beginning and made visible in human form over two thousand years ago.

When you use a word, you attempt to name and capture a reality in order to communicate with someone else. The word "elephant," for example, names a particular pachyderm and attempts to capture the reality of the animal. But words are deficient. They are not capable of communicating the totality of the reality which they name. There is more to an elephant than just its name—there is its size, its texture, its smell, and its sound. When all is said and done, the name "elephant" communicates little about the animal.

When we call Jesus the "Word of God," we discover our deficiency and confront God's power. All the Lord has to do is speak a word and the reality is created. Jesus is the incarnate God. He showed us God in human flesh—flesh that could be heard, seen, and touched. It is this Word which is spoken from the ambo. It is this Word to whom you listen in order to nourish your spirit.

Meditation:

How does the Word of God nourish your spirit? What are some of your favorite words? What reality does each attempt to describe? How is each deficient?

Prayer:

O Lord, your word is a lamp that gives light wherever I walk. Your laws are fair, and I have given my word to respect them all (Psalm 119:105-106).

Memories:

What are some of your favorite biblical passages that nourish your spirit?

Chair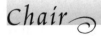

Scripture:

Jesus said to the crowds and to his disciples: "The Pharisees and the teachers of the Law are experts in the Law of Moses. So obey everything they teach you, but don't do as they do. After all, they say one thing and do something else" (Matthew 23:1-3).

Reflection:

Those who are experts usually occupy a chair, a seat of authority or honor, such as the concert master of a symphony orchestra, a teacher at a university, or a board chairperson. When kings and queens hold court or call parliament into session, they sit in large chairs. Likewise, the pope often speaks sitting in a big chair.

In the parish church where the bishop is pastor, called a cathedral—from the Greek word for chair, "cathedra"—there is a large chair from which he presides over his diocese. Every parish church contains a smaller version of the bishop's chair—called the presidential or presider's chair—where the bishop's representative leads a local parish.

Chairs in our homes function as signs of authority or honor, too. "That's dad's chair," a child might tell an adult visitor about to sit in what the youngster identifies as his or her father's favorite. Likewise, around the dining room table you can find one or two chairs with arms, often referred to as the captain's chairs. Parents usually sit in those chairs. When an elderly relative comes to visit, the best chair in your house may be offered to him or her.

Meditation:

From what chairs in your home do you exercise authority? In what chairs are you honored?

Prayer:

Our LORD, I will sing of your love forever. Everyone yet to be born will hear me praise your faithfulness. Your kingdom is ruled by justice and fairness with love and faithfulness leading the way. Your own glorious power makes us strong, and because of your kindness, our strength increases (Psalm 89:1, 14, 17).

MEMORIES:

Make a list of the different types of chairs you find in your home, at work, and in church. For each, identify the authority or honor it represents.

Jesus of Nazareth

SCRIPTURE:

The angel said, "Joseph, the baby that Mary will have is from the Holy Spirit. Go ahead and marry her. Then after her baby is born, name him Jesus, because he will save his people from their sins" (Matthew 1:20-21).

REFLECTION:

Sometime between 6 and 4 B.C. Jesus was born; sometime around 30 A.D. he died on a cross. The man who was known as Jesus of Nazareth lived thirty-plus years on the third planet from the sun. Meaning "Yahweh helps" or "Yahweh saves," Jesus' name refers to the historical person who bore it.

The historical life of Jesus is attested in both the New Testament and in Christian and non-Christian writings of the first and second century. This Jesus of history is the one whom we Christians proclaim to be, in the words of Peter in Matthew's gospel, "the Messiah, the Son of the living God" (Matthew 16:16). The name "Christ" is a Greek word meaning "anointed" and is a translation of the Hebrew word "Messiah." Because we believe that God raised Jesus from the dead, we declare Jesus to be God's anointed, the Christ, who saved the world from its sins.

Sometimes we have a tendency to forget that Jesus was a real historical person, human like us in every way but sin. During Lent, we focus on the historical Jesus, the man who was tempted, drove moneychangers from the temple, told parables about forgiveness, suffered, and died on the cross. During Easter we focus on the risen Jesus whom we proclaim as Christ, the one who appeared to his disciples in Jerusalem, on the way to Emmaus, and near the Sea of Tiberias.

Meditation:

Can you distinguish the Jesus of history from the Christ of faith? Do you focus more on the Jesus of history or the Christ of faith?

Prayer:

Christ was humble. He obeyed God and even died on a cross. Then God gave Christ the highest place and honored his name above all others. So at the name of Jesus everyone will bow down, those in heaven, on earth, and under the earth. And to the glory of God the Father everyone will openly agree, "Jesus Christ is Lord!" (Philippians 2:8-11).

Identify your favorite statue, painting, stained-glass window, sculpture, etc. of Jesus. Does it focus more on the humanity or divinity of Jesus?

Exodus

SCRIPTURE:

Suddenly Moses and Elijah were there speaking with Jesus. They appeared in heavenly glory and talked about all that Jesus' death in Jerusalem would mean (Luke 9:30-31).

REFLECTION:

Every year on the Second Sunday of Lent we hear an account of Jesus' transfiguration. Only Luke's version notes that Moses and Elijah talked about Jesus' death, his departure, his exodus in Jerusalem. Thus, only Luke understands Jesus' death to be like the hasty departure of the Israelites out of Egypt, their liberation from slavery.

In the oldest account of the transfiguration, found in Mark's Gospel—which has no post-resurrection account—the story tells the reader that God will raise Jesus from the dead. Luke's rewritten version understands resurrection as an exodus, a passage through death to life.

We are always in the process of "exodusing," of leaving behind and moving on. We make an exodus every year from one age to another. Who we are at fifty is not who we were at twenty-five. Or maybe you moved out of a large house and into a smaller house or an apartment. If you have, you probably gave away or left behind a lot of possessions and old familiar ways of doing things. That's what an exodus calls us to do, to leave behind what we don't need and to march forward into deeper, transfigured life.

Meditation:

What has been your most recent exodus? What did you leave behind? To where did you move?

Prayer:

Look deep into my heart, God, and find out everything I am thinking. Don't let me follow evil ways, but lead me in the way that time has proven true (Psalm 139:23-24).

Memories:

What lifetime exodus was your most transfiguring experience? When and where did it take place? Who was involved? How were you changed?

Wine

Scripture:

Jesus took a cup of wine in his hands and gave thanks to God. Then he told the apostles, "Take this wine and share it with each other. I tell you that I will not drink any more wine until God's kingdom comes." After the meal he took another cup of wine in his hands. Then he said, "This is my blood. It is poured out for you, and with it God makes his new agreement" (Luke 22:17-18, 20).

Reflection:

Only in Luke's Gospel does the narrator tell the reader that Jesus takes two cups of wine. After the first cup, Jesus says that he will not drink wine again until the fullness of God's reign is present. After the second cup, Jesus explains that the wine represents his blood, the blood of the new covenant, another unique feature of Luke's Gospel. Both Mark and Matthew understand that Jesus' blood is a continuation of the covenant God entered into with Moses, not a new covenant.

Red wine represents blood. In the Passover celebration, it represents the blood of the lamb smeared on the lintel and doorposts of the Hebrews' homes. But in the new Passover feast, it represents the blood of Christ, shed on the cross for the whole world. And when Christians gather to celebrate eucharist, it represents all the times they have poured out themselves in love for others.

Wine is one of the finer things in life. On special occasions it is shared among families in homes. The bottle is uncorked and the liquid poured into glasses, which are touched together as a sign of the family unity being commemorated by the gathering. During Lent and Easter, we focus on the unity wine engenders as we share our gifts with others and drink from the cup of salvation, recognizing that we are in the cup as the blood of Christ.

Meditation:

In what ways have you been poured out in service to others in the past few days? How do these flow from and lead you back to sharing from the cup of the blood of Christ in eucharist?

Prayer:

What must I give you, LORD, for being so good to me? I will pour out an offering of wine to you, and I will pray in your name because you have saved me. I will keep my promise to you when your people meet (Psalm 116:12-14).

Memories:

At what special family gatherings do you share wine? Make a list and identify how the wine helps create a unity among those present.

Tomb

Scripture:

In the place where Jesus had been nailed to a cross, there was a garden with a tomb that had never been used. The tomb was nearby, and since it was the time to prepare for the Sabbath, [Joseph from Arimathea and Nicodemus] were in a hurry to put Jesus' body there (John 19:41-42).

Reflection:

In the ancient world many tombs were caves with shelves carved out of the walls. The body of the deceased would be washed, anointed with myrrh, and wrapped in a shroud with spices placed both in and out. After a couple of years, the flesh would decompose and the bones would be collected and stored in a clay jar or box, called an ossuary, and placed under the shelf, which could be used for the next family member to die. Thus, such tombs would be used by generations of the same family.

Today we usually refer to a burial place as a grave, a six foot hole in the ground. The grave is the destination of the funeral procession and is often described as the deceased's place of rest. Around graves we gather to remember and honor the dead on Memorial Day, Veterans Day, and All Souls' Day.

Usually thought of as places of death, tombs and graves are really gardens of life for those who believe that God raised Jesus from the dead and will do the same for us. Only John's Gospel states that Jesus' tomb was located in a garden. Through this little detail, John anticipates the rest of his story, the resurrection. What Joseph from Arimathea and Nicodemus identified as death, God saw as life awakening in a garden, just like in the beginning in the garden of paradise.

Meditation:

What family members' graves do you visit on a regular basis? Why do you visit them? How do you honor the memory of those buried there?

Each day I lift my hands in prayer to you, LORD. Do you work miracles for the dead? Do they stand up and praise you? Are your love and loyalty announced in the world of the dead? Do they know of your miracles or your saving power in the dark world below where all is forgotten? Each morning I pray to you, LORD (Psalm 88:9-13).

MEMORIES:

Make a list of your family members who have died (great-grandparents, grandparents, parents, etc.) and for each indicate where his or her grave is located.

Death

SCRIPTURE:

You died, which means that your life is hidden with Christ, who sits beside God (Colossians 3:3).

REFLECTION:

Jesus died. You will die. In a culture that fears death as much as ours, a healthy appreciation for the end of life as we know it is difficult to achieve. Through closed caskets, immediate cremation, and private burial, we get further and further away from the reality of death. And we fear it more and more.

That's why we spend some time during Lent focusing on death. "Remember, you are dust and to dust you will return," the minister tells you on Ash Wednesday while crossing your forehead with ashes, a sign of your mortality. For those who believe that God raised Jesus from the dead, death should not be feared. It is a passageway from this life to eternal life. Death is a passover from life to life. Through death, life is changed, but it is not ended. As a member of his body, our new life is hidden with Christ.

We are given a lifetime to practice death, to remind ourselves that we are not here to stay, but merely passing through. Every time we let go of control, manipulation of another, a grudge, a hurt, etc., we die. And such mini-deaths are preludes to how well we can take our last breath and cross over to a life hidden in Christ.

Meditation:

What is your greatest fear about death? What is your greatest hope?

Prayer:

How much longer, LORD? Will you hide forever? Remember, life is short! Why did you empty our lives of all meaning? No one can escape the power of death and the grave (Psalm 89:46-48).

Memories:

Make a list of your closest relatives who have died. For each, indicate what experiences of their lives helped to prepare them for death.

Holy Week

Holy Week

SCRIPTURE:

A week later the disciples were together again. This time, Thomas was with them. Jesus came in while the doors were still locked and stood in the middle of the group (John 20:26).

REFLECTION:

The traditional understanding of Holy Week is that it begins on Passion (Palm) Sunday and ends on Easter Sunday. But there is another Holy Week that begins on Easter Sunday and ends the Sunday following. Both of these weeks consist of eight days.

In our way of computing time, we begin with zero. Thus, from Sunday (zero) at noon to Monday at noon is one full day. But in Jewish understanding—before zero was invented—from Sunday noon to Monday noon was understood as two days. Thus, from one Sunday to the next Sunday is an octave or eight days.

The eight days of Passion (Palm) Sunday to Easter Sunday and the eight days of Easter Sunday to the Second Sunday of Easter each form an octave, a Holy Week of completeness, fullness, a new beginning. During the former Holy Week, we travel from Jesus' victorious entrance into Jerusalem to his resurrection. During the latter Holy Week, we travel with Thomas from doubt to faith.

Meditation:

How does your observance of Holy Week bring you to completeness, fullness, and a new beginning?

Prayer:

Shout praises to the LORD! With all my heart I will thank the LORD when his people meet. Respect and obey the LORD! This is the first step to wisdom and good sense. God will always be respected (Psalm 111:1, 10).

Memories:

Last year, how did you observe Holy Week? How do you intend to observe Holy Week this year?

Palms

Scripture:

The next day a large crowd was in Jerusalem for Passover. When they heard that Jesus was coming for the festival, they took palm branches and went out to greet him. They shouted, "Hooray! God bless the one who comes in the name of the Lord! God bless the King of Israel!" (John 12:12-13).

Reflection:

The ashes smudged in the sign of a cross on our foreheads on Ash Wednesday come from the leftover and burned palms of the previous year's Passion (Palm) Sunday celebration. Those two days are tied together with dust! Ashes from palm branches remind us of our lifetime journey to death, and through it, to eternal life.

The palm branch, a sign of victory, used to welcome great conquerors in the ancient world, was once flexible, green, and alive before it was stripped from the tree. But once it begins to dry, it becomes stiff, brown, and dead. One day, you will become the ashes of the palm.

Only in John's Gospel does the crowd greet Jesus with palm fronds. Mark, Matthew, and Luke tell us that the crowd spread cloaks on the road or cut branches from trees. But the cheers of the crowd quickly end in a blood bath. Victory, life, is achieved only through death, dust.

Meditation:

During your life, what victories have you achieved through death, dust?

Prayer:

The LORD is our God, and he has given us light! Start the celebration! March with palm branches all the way to the altar. The LORD is my God! I will praise him and tell him how thankful I am (Psalm 118:27-28).

What do you do with the palm branches you bring home from church on Passion (Palm) Sunday?

(Easter) Triduum

SCRIPTURE:

Jesus said, ". . . The Son of Man will be deep in the earth for three days and nights" (Matthew 12:40).

REFLECTION:

"Triduum" is a Latin word meaning "three days." Thus, the Easter Triduum consists of three days, each beginning and ending at sunset. The first day begins at sunset on Holy Thursday and lasts until sunset on Good Friday. Then, from Good Friday sunset to Holy Saturday sunset is the second day. The third day begins at sunset on Holy Saturday and ends with sunset on Easter Sunday.

Three is a sacred biblical number signaling a theophany, a sudden appearance of God. Abraham receives three visitors in the heat of the day and discovers that God has come to tell him and Sarah that they will have a son, Isaac. Gideon offers three measures of flour and witnesses God's fire not only consuming his offering, but naming him a judge of Israel. Likewise, barren Hannah promises God that she will dedicate her child to God if God will give her a son. She offers three measures of flour and conceives and gives birth to Samuel, the anointer of Israel's first kings—Saul and David.

Jonah, who spent three days and nights in the belly of the big fish, becomes a prototype for Jesus' three days and nights in the tomb. Just as God's words were effective through Jonah to the people of Nineveh, so were God's words effective through Jesus to the people of all time. After three days, Jonah was spewed out of the fish onto the seashore and he knew that he had encountered God. Christ danced out of the grave after three days and God manifested the divine presence once again.

MEDITATION:

Name a recent theophany in your life. Was the biblical number three involved in your experience in any way? How?

PRAYER:

The LORD is my fortress! The LORD is sitting in his sacred temple on his throne in heaven. He knows everything we do because he sees us all. The LORD always does right and wants justice done. Everyone who does right will see his face (Psalm 11:1, 4, 7).

MEMORIES:

Examine some of your life experiences of the divine presence and determine how many of them are associated with the number three. How was each a theophany, an experience of God?

Feet

Scripture:

During the meal Jesus got up, removed his outer garment, and wrapped a towel around his waist. He put some water into a large bowl. Then he began washing his disciples' feet and drying them with the towel he was wearing (John 13:4-5).

Reflection:

Feet are necessary for walking, running, jogging, pedaling, hiking, stomping, etc. Being the lowest part of the human body and usually clothed with socks and shoes, we think of our feet less often than we do our hands. While bare feet are acceptable on the beach and, maybe, at home, covered feet are required in most public places, especially those displaying a "No Shirt, No Shoes, No Service" sign.

In Jesus' time, most homes welcomed visitors with a pitcher of water, a basin, and a towel. After walking the dusty streets and roads in sandals, one's feet needed washing. So, inside the foyer a person could find what was necessary to cleanse his or her feet.

According to John's Gospel, Jesus makes foot-washing a sign of service. He engages in an activity that no one could be forced to do—wash another person's feet. Willingly, he takes the water and towel and, kneeling at his disciples' feet, humiliates himself. When finished, he tells them that all are equal—equal foot-washers. That's the kind of service to which every person is called.

Meditation:

Whose feet have you recently washed? How did you wash him or her? What kind of Christian service did you provide?

Prayer:

I patiently waited, LORD, for you to hear my prayer. You listened and pulled me from a lonely pit full of mud and mire. You let me stand on a rock with my feet firm, and you gave me a new song, a song of praise to you (Psalm 40:1-3).

Memories:

Make a list of the important places your feet have taken you. For each place indicate what kind of service you gave or received there.

(Holy) Thursday

Scripture:

It was the first day of the Festival of Thin Bread, and the Passover lambs were being killed. Jesus' disciples . . . went into the city and . . . prepared the Passover meal. While Jesus and the twelve disciples were eating together that evening . . . Jesus took some bread in his hands. He blessed the bread and broke it. Then he gave it to his disciples and said, "Take this. It is my body." Jesus picked up a cup of wine and gave thanks to God. He gave it to his disciples, and they all drank some. Then he said, "This is my blood, which is poured out for many people, and with it God makes his agreement" (Mark 14:12, 16-17, 22-24).

Reflection:

Sometime after four in the afternoon on Holy Thursday, three days before Easter Sunday, people gather to remember Jesus' Last Supper with his disciples. It was a Passover meal during which, using signs, he reinterpreted the two primary symbols of Passover—bread and wine.

Instead of the thin, unleavened bread of Passover calling to mind the Israelites' hurried escape from Egypt, henceforth it would be a reminder of Jesus' body, broken and shared. Instead of the cup of wine of Passover recalling the blood of the covenant sealed between God and the Israelites when Moses sprinkled blood on the altar and on them, hereafter it would be a reminder of Jesus' blood, poured out in love.

Sometimes called Maundy Thursday ("Maundy" comes from the Latin "mandatum," meaning "mandate" or "order"), the day's focus is on service. Jesus served his body and blood to his followers. We continue to break the bread of his body and share the cup of his blood every time we serve others, both those in and those out of the Christian community.

Meditation:

How does the Lord's Supper give you a mandate to serve others?

Our LORD, by your wisdom you made so many things; the whole earth is covered with your living creatures. All of these depend on you to provide them with food, and you feed each one with your own hand, until they are full. As long as I live, I will sing and praise you, the LORD God (Psalm 104:24, 27-28, 33).

MEMORIES:

What was your most memorable Holy Thursday? What made it so?

(Good) Friday

SCRIPTURE:

The next day would be both a Sabbath and the Passover. It was a special day for the Jewish people, and they did not want the bodies to stay on the crosses during that day (John 19:31).

REFLECTION:

The sixth day of the week, the day when Jesus died, is described ironically as good. It is "good" because we can face death with faith that what God did for Jesus—raise him to new life—God will do for us.

So, on Good Friday we celebrate the Lord's passion, his suffering, and death. We do not pretend that Jesus has just died or that this is his funeral. By remembering Jesus' suffering and death on the cross through scripture readings, prayers, adoration of the cross, and communion, we realize that our suffering and death have been made holy by him. Indeed, all of our experiences can be vehicles for the manifestation of God's presence in our life.

With Joseph from Arimathea and Nicodemus in John's Gospel, we escort the body of Jesus to its garden tomb. Unlike them, we face the sealed tomb with faith in new and eternal life.

Meditation:

How is Good Friday "good" to and for you?

Prayer:

I praise you, LORD! I prayed, and you rescued me. Death had wrapped its ropes around me, and I was almost swallowed by its flooding waters. I was in terrible trouble when I called out to you, but from your temple you heard me and answered my prayer (Psalm 18:3-4, 6).

Memories:

What especially memorable Good Friday can you recall? What made it so special to you?

(Holy) Saturday

SCRIPTURE:

It was now the evening before the Sabbath, and the Jewish people were getting ready for that sacred day (Mark 15:42).

REFLECTION:

In Jesus' day, the Sabbath was the last day of the week, Saturday—not the first day of the week, Sunday, like it is for Christians. The Jews rested the last day of the week because God had stopped working on the Sabbath. Such a rest is what best characterizes Holy Saturday today. After all, it is Jesus' Sabbath day.

On Holy Saturday nothing goes on in church, maybe except for some decorating. The silence we experience on this Saturday is like that when we stand beside the grave of a loved one who has died and been buried. We remember all the good times we shared with the person and realize that we will never enjoy his or her company again.

On this day of preparation for baptism, confirmation, and eucharist by catechumens, all engage in Sabbath observance. Then, in the midst of such emptiness, after darkness descends on the earth, we begin the Easter Vigil. A fire lights up the darkness. A minister declares that Christ has risen. Alleluia resounds. And those who are ready are washed, anointed, and come to the Lord's table.

Meditation:

How do you usually observe Holy Saturday? What could you do to make a more prayerful and silent experience in preparation for the Easter Vigil?

Prayer:

The stone that the builders tossed aside has now become the most important stone. The LORD has done this, and it is amazing to us. This day belongs to the LORD! Let's celebrate and be glad today. We'll ask the LORD to save us! We'll sincerely ask the LORD to let us win (Psalm 118:22-25).

Memories:

What has been your most memorable observance of Holy Saturday? What made it so?

Easter

Easter (Sunday)

Scripture:

Peter said: "Now I am certain that God treats all people alike. God is pleased with everyone who worships him and does right, no matter what nation they come from" (Acts 10:34-35).

Reflection:

Easter Sunday is not named for Christ's resurrection. Easter comes from "Easter," the name for the goddess of dawn whose spring festival was celebrated near the Jewish commemoration of passover, another feast associated with spring. The Christian celebration of Christ's resurrection always falls on the first Sunday following the first full moon that occurs on or after March 21, the spring equinox.

Since we do not know of what resurrected life consists, we mark Easter Sunday with signs of resurrection. The day is filled with eggs, from which come baby chickens; baskets filled with foods that give us life; new clothes, reminders of the new life of Christ which we put on the day we were baptized.

But there is more to this day than Easter egg hunts, candy, and new threads. Easter means that God shows no partiality. By raising Jesus from the dead, God demonstrates that God is interested in all people and chooses all people to share in the resurrected life of Christ.

What does Easter mean for you? Why do you think Easter is always celebrated on a Sunday in the spring?

Prayer:

He made the bright lights in the sky. God's love never fails. He lets the sun rule each day. God's love never fails. He lets the moon and the stars rule each night. God's love never fails (Psalm 136:7-9).

Memories:

What items do you display in your home for Easter? Make a list of them and indicate what each represents for you.

(Easter) Vigil

Scripture:

Moses called the leaders of Israel together and said: "Your children will ask you, 'What are we celebrating?' And you will answer, 'The Passover animal is killed to honor the LORD. We do these things because on that night long ago the LORD passed over the homes of our people in Egypt. He killed the first-born sons of the Egyptians, but he saved our children from death'" (Exodus 12:21, 26-27).

Reflection:

A vigil is a watch during the night, usually in preparation for an important feast or occasion. Most people don't call a sleepless night a vigil, but in a sense that is what it is, especially if it precedes a graduation, a marriage, or the beginning of an important business trip. Religious people often spend all night or part of a night in prayer before a special feast in honor of God.

Such is the Easter Vigil. Beginning after sunset on Holy Saturday, people enter into prayer and song, awaiting Easter Sunday and the proclamation of Christ's resurrection. Indeed, the Easter Vigil explodes with signs of the resurrection. Beginning with a fire outside the church, the Easter Candle, a sign of the risen Christ, is lit. Then, the pilgrimage is made into the church with the light of Christ leading the way. There, Scripture readings are heard that trace the presence of God's light and love with us since the beginning of time.

The high point of the Easter Vigil is the baptism of catechumens, those who have been preparing to enter into the death and resurrection of Christ through baptism. After being washed, anointed with chrism, and welcomed, they join the rest of the assembly in eating and drinking from the Lord's table—bread and wine—signs of Christ risen for the first time. We do these things because on a night long ago God raised Christ from the dead and nothing has been the same since.

Meditation:

When have you recently entered into a vigil? For what were you preparing?

Our LORD, in all generations you have been our home. You have always been God—long before the birth of the mountains, even before you created the earth and the world. At your command we die and turn back to dust, but a thousand years mean nothing to you! They are merely a day gone by or a few hours in the night (Psalm 90:1-4).

MEMORIES:

What is your most memorable Easter Vigil? What made it so?

(Easter) Sunday

SCRIPTURE:

After the Sabbath, Mary Magdalene, Salome, and Mary the mother of James bought some spices to put on Jesus' body. Very early on Sunday morning, just as the sun was coming up, they went to the tomb (Mark 16:1-2).

REFLECTION:

Faith in the resurrection of Jesus is the foundation of Christianity. Attempts to capture the truth of the resurrection are always metaphorical. We say the resurrection is "like this" or "like that," but we cannot capture its richness in words. Even the word "resurrection" is a metaphor. Literally, the word means "to rise again," implying that one has risen before—as in rising every morning from one's bed. Therefore, resurrection must be like rising from a bed (the tomb where Jesus slept for three days).

On Easter Sunday, Christian faith reaches its peak. In fact, it can't be contained in only one day. It spills over into all fifty-two Sundays of the year. It takes a whole year to mine its richness. Thus, every Sunday is a little Easter, a mini-celebration flowing from Easter Sunday.

On the first Easter Sunday, after observing the Sabbath rest, the women bring spices to Jesus' tomb before the usual work of the day begins. They come at sunrise on the sun's day—Sunday. Their greeting of the dawning light is another metaphor for resurrection. Christ, the light of the world, has risen. And the brightness of his glory transforms the grief of death to the amazement of new life.

Meditation:

In what ways do you observe every Sunday as a little Easter, one filled with new life?

Prayer:

Let the name of the LORD be praised now and forever. From dawn until sunset the name of the LORD deserves to be praised. The LORD is far above all of the nations; he is more glorious than the heavens (Psalm 113:2-4).

Memories:

What is your most memorable Easter Sunday celebration? What made it so?

Kindling

SCRIPTURE:

The LORD immediately sent fire, and it burned up the sacrifice, the wood, and the stones. It scorched the ground everywhere around the altar and dried up every drop of water in the ditch. When the crowd saw what had happened, they all bowed down and shouted, "The LORD is God! The LORD is God!" (1 Kings 18:38-39).

REFLECTION:

The Easter Vigil begins sometime after sunset on Holy Saturday and is conducted before sunrise Easter Sunday morning. It begins with a large fire kindled outside the church around which all gather. To build a suitable fire, pieces of wood are needed, including kindling.

The fire signifies the new light and life of Christ's resurrection. It represents Christ, the light of the world. It inflames with new hope those who feel its heat and see its warmth. The fire also points toward the purification we have received through the waters of baptism and our observance of Lent.

Throughout the Old Testament, God is often represented by fire. Moses encounters God in a burning bush. Gideon's sacrifice is devoured by flames. Elijah's sacrifice is consumed by God's fire along with the wood used for the fire, the stones used to build the altar, and the water in the trench around the altar!

In what ways have you encountered God through fire?

From east to west, the powerful LORD God has been calling together everyone on earth. God shines brightly. Our God approaches, but not silently; a flaming fire comes first, and a storm surrounds him (Psalm 50:1-3).

When you have attended the Easter Vigil, have you experienced a fire being kindled? What made it memorable for you?

Baptism

Scripture:

Jesus [told Nicodemus], "I tell you for certain that before you can get into God's kingdom, you must be born not only by water, but by the Spirit" (John 3:5).

Reflection:

The Greek word for baptism, "baptizein," means to immerse in water. Originally referring to immersing fabric in dye, the word became specifically associated with Jewish ritual washing, especially among the Essenes, to signify a person's cleanliness or purity before God. Christians practiced immersion as a rite of initiation, a ceremony of welcoming a person as a member of the community.

Lent focuses on baptism in two ways. First, the catechumens, those preparing for baptism during the Easter Vigil, enter into the last days and stages of initiation. They are chosen by the community for baptism, given the Lord's Prayer and the Creed, and anointed with oil. Every day of Lent they step closer to the baptismal font.

Second, Lent prepares those of us already baptized to renew our baptismal promises during the Easter Vigil. We, the initiators of the catechumens, are reminded of our baptism by water, the baptismal font in our church, the scriptures, our godparents or sponsors, etc. After the catechumens have declared their faith in the triune God, they are baptized during the Easter Vigil. We too, born of water and the Spirit, profess our faith and are sprinkled with water.

Meditation:

What does your baptism mean to you? How do you live it daily?

Prayer:

You are kind, God! Please have pity on me. You are always merciful! Please wipe away my sins.

Wash me clean from all of my sin and guilt. Let me be happy and joyful! (Psalm 51:1-2, 8).

Memories:

What is the date of your baptism? Put it on your calendar and celebrate it.

Font

Scripture:

Don't you know that all who share in Christ Jesus by being baptized also share in his death? When we were baptized, we died and were buried with Christ. We were baptized, so that we would live a new life, as Christ was raised to life by the glory of God the Father (Romans 6:3-4).

Reflection:

If you go to an old parish church, the baptismal font will most likely consist of some type of stand with a basin or bowl filled with water. In new or redesigned churches it is usually a fountain or a pool of water into which a person can be immersed.

In the ancient world, the baptistery was a separate room into which a grave-like rectangle had been cut out of the floor and filled with water. On one side of this grave, those who were ready to be baptized shed all their clothes, walked down the three steps into the dark waters, were immersed or drowned, rose, and walked up the three steps on the other side. There, they were clothed in a white garment, anointed with sweet-smelling perfume, and led to the church to meet the other baptized members.

In the watery grave a person died, just like Christ died and was buried in the tomb. On the other side of the grave a person rose, just as God had raised Jesus from the dead. Thus, the tomb was also a womb. In it life ceased and life was quickened. The day of your baptism is more important than the day of your birth. St. Augustine called the baptismal font the womb of the church, since from this womb all God's children are born. Your new life began in the baptismal font.

Meditation:

How do you live your baptismal death and resurrection? Recall several recent experiences of dying and rising to new life.

Prayer:

Our LORD, I will remember the things you have done, your miracles of long ago. You walked through the water of the mighty sea, but your footprints were never seen. You guided your people like a flock of sheep (Psalm 77:11, 19-20).

Memories:

In what type of font were you baptized? Where is the font located? If possible, make a trip to see the font and remember that your new life began in it.

Water

SCRIPTURE:

The angel showed me a river that was crystal clear, and its waters gave life. The river came from the throne where God and the Lamb were seated. If you are thirsty, come! If you want life-giving water, come and take it. It's free! (Revelation 22:1, 17).

REFLECTION:

We pay little attention to the water in our kitchen sink, in our bathroom sink, shower, and toilet, and in our utility room washer until it is turned off. Likewise, we pay little attention to the water in our lakes until we see a sign that tells us it is dangerous to swim in them. For years now, people all around the world have been attempting to clean up the industrial-polluted water in our lakes and rivers.

Water is the stream of life. In biblical literature it is often employed as a metaphor for grace, God's own life that God shares with thirsty people. If we think of grace as an action of God or the process of God sharing who God is with us, we more readily see why the author of the Book of Revelation invites us to drink from the stream flowing from God's throne. After all, it's free.

During Lent, the catechumens prepare to be immersed in the water of baptism, and those already baptized prepare to renew their baptismal promises. During the fifty days of Easter, we can place a bowl of water on our dining room table or someplace else easily seen and accessible. Before or after meals each person can dip a hand in the water and remember his or her baptism, the day God's grace flooded his or her life.

Recall the body of water to which you live closest. Is it an ocean, a lake, a river, a creek, a small stream? Using it as a metaphor for grace, in what ways has God given you life?

Prayer:

As a deer gets thirsty for streams of water, I truly am thirsty for you, my God. In my heart, I am thirsty for you, the living God. When will I see your face? I trust you! And I will praise you again because you help me, and you are my God (Psalm 42:1-2, 5-6).

Memories:

Make a list of the bodies of water you have seen, swam in, skied on, boated on, etc. When finished, ask yourself, "What do my experiences of water teach me about my relationship with God?"

Oils

Scripture:

Jesus was eating in Bethany at the home of Simon, who once had leprosy, when a woman came in with a very expensive bottle of sweet-smelling perfume. After breaking it open, she poured the perfume on Jesus' head (Mark 14:3).

Reflection:

Usually displayed or kept near the baptismal font in churches are three oils—chrism, the Oil of Catechumens, and the Oil of the Sick. Chrism gets its name from Christ, which means "Anointed." Whoever is anointed with chrism is "Christed," that is, he or she is sealed with the Holy Spirit in baptism, confirmation, and holy orders and designated one of God's chosen people.

With the Oil of Catechumens, ministers anoint those who are being taught the fundamentals of and formed in the tradition of the church in preparation for initiation. Catechumens are strengthened to persevere in their developing faith and the lifestyle it demands.

The ill are anointed with the Oil of the Sick, imploring God, if God wills, to heal them. Healing need not be confined to physical illness, but might involve the emotional healing needed after childhood abuse, the spiritual healing needed after neglecting faith, or the psychological healing needed after chemical dependency.

Meditation:

How do your actions demonstrate that you are an anointed one, another Christ? In what ways has God strengthened you during the past year? Of what has God healed you in the past year?

Prayer:

It is truly wonderful when relatives live together in peace. It is as beautiful as olive oil poured on Aaron's head and running down his beard and the collar of his robe. It is like the dew from Mount Hermon, falling on Zion's mountains, where the LORD has promised to bless his people with life forevermore (Psalm 133:1-3).

Prepare a record of when you have been anointed with chrism (baptism, confirmation, ordination to the priesthood or episcopacy), Oil of Catechumens (before baptism), and the Oil of the Sick (before surgery or during treatment for a disease).

(Easter) Candle

S c r i p t u r e :

Jesus told us that God is light and doesn't have any darkness in him. Now we are telling you (1 John 1:5).

R e f l e c t i o n :

Except during the Easter Season, the Easter Candle, a large pillar of wax, stands near the baptismal font in church. When it is lit from the Easter Vigil fire and carried into church, the minister sings, "Christ our light," to indicate that not only is Christ risen, but he continues to lead people on their pilgrimage of faith.

After you were baptized, you received a small candle lit from the Easter Candle. Your candle indicates that you have been raised from the dead and that you are now God's light shining in the world. Because God is immaterial, we often speak of God as being light. The followers of Jesus should be material light.

While a candle brightens up a room, sets a mood for a gathering of friends, or adds atmosphere to a table in a restaurant, its purpose is complete when its fire burns all its wax. Our purpose is to burn with the light of God until the day we die.

Meditation:

What are some of the important experiences of your pilgrimage of faith? How was your light shining?

Prayer:

You, LORD, are the light that keeps me safe. I am not afraid of anyone. You protect me, and I have no fears (Psalm 27:1).

Memories:

If you have your baptismal candle, locate it and light it on the anniversary of your baptism. If you don't have one, purchase a candle, put your name on it and the date of your baptism, and light it on your baptismal anniversary.

White Garment

Scripture:

. . . I saw a large crowd with more people than could be counted. They were from every race, tribe, nation, and language, and they stood before the throne and before the Lamb. They wore white robes and held palm branches in their hands . . . (Revelation 7:9).

Reflection:

Every morning, after showering, we get dressed and begin our usual activities. While some thought goes into what clothes we will wear, most of us just open the closet and decide. Of course, more thought is given to dressing up for a special occasion, like a graduation, a wedding, a funeral, etc. We don't think about it all that much, but we realize that the clothes we wear indicate not only our own importance, but also how we value the solemnity of the occasion.

This sign-value of clothes is operative in the Book of Revelation. In John's vision, those standing before the throne dressed in long white robes and holding palm branches in their hands are the Christians who have died for their faith. Their white robe signifies their baptism and the palm branch indicates that they were both martyred and victorious.

Once catechumens are baptized during the Easter Vigil, each is clothed in a white garment. Not only does the garment signify their purity and newness, but it also represents their status as members of the "crowd," described in Revelation as the body of Christ, men and women from every race, nation, culture, and language, and their sharing in everlasting life.

Meditation:

In what ways do your clothes disclose who you are and what you consider to be important in life?

Prayer:

I praise you, LORD God, with all my heart. You are glorious and majestic, dressed in royal robes

and surrounded by light. Our LORD, we pray
that your glory will last forever and that you will
be pleased with what you have done. As long as
I live, I will sing and praise you, the LORD God
(Psalm 104:1-2, 31, 33).

MEMORIES:

Where is the white garment you received when
you were baptized or the clothes you wore when
you were baptized? If possible, retrieve them or
get a photograph of yourself in them to remind
you of who you are in Christ.

Clothes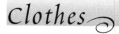

SCRIPTURE:

Jesus said to his disciples: "Look how the wild
flowers grow! They don't work hard to make
their clothes. But I tell you that Solomon with
all his wealth wasn't as well clothed as one of
these flowers" (Luke 12:22, 27).

REFLECTION:

As far as I am concerned, there is nothing more beautiful
than a prairie or mountain meadow blanketed with wild
flowers. Granted, it takes a while to get used to the smaller
flowers in a culture that always boasts bigger is better,
even in bouquets. But once the tiny elegance of an orchid
or lily or daisy is appreciated, King Solomon's
well-woven and dyed purple royal robes pale in
comparison.

Many people observe an Easter custom of buying new clothes in remembrance of the new white garment received after baptism. We feel different when we put on a new shirt and tie or blouse, a new pair of jeans, a new suit or dress. The old song about putting on a new Easter bonnet captures the same feeling from a time when women wore bonnets or hats.

But there is more to putting on new clothes than just dressing ourselves in clean garments. What we put on reminds us that we have also put on Christ. The way we live our lives demonstrates that we have put on faith in his resurrection. And that makes the best of clothes to wear.

Meditation:

In what ways do your clothes reflect your Christian way of life?

Prayer:

You have turned my sorrow into joyful dancing. No longer am I sad and wearing sackcloth. I thank you from my heart, and I will never stop singing your praises, my LORD and my God (Psalm 30:11-12).

Memories:

What new clothes do you remember buying for Easters past?

Passover

SCRIPTURE:

Because of his faith, Moses left Egypt. Moses had seen the invisible God and wasn't afraid of the king's anger. His faith also made him celebrate Passover. He sprinkled the blood of animals on the doorposts, so that the first-born sons of the people of Israel would not be killed by the destroying angel (Hebrews 11:27-28).

REFLECTION:

Passover is all about facing imminent death and ending up alive. Without the blood of the lamb on their doorposts, the Hebrews faced imminent death from the destroying angel, but with the blood they came out alive. Without the pillar of fire, the Hebrews faced imminent death from Pharaoh's army, but with it passing over them they came out alive.

After arriving at the Sea of Reeds, the people face imminent death again. But God parts the sea and they pass through its midst and come out alive on the opposite shore. After crossing the Jordan River into the promised land, a mini-exodus, Joshua instructs the Israelites to remember that they have been saved from imminent death and been given life by celebrating the Passover.

Jesus, too, passed over. He faced his imminent death and passed over it to resurrected life. And what he has done, he invites us to do. Lent and Easter call us to reflect on all the passover experiences of our lives because these contain the resources we need to confidently enter into death with the faith that we will pass over to eternal life.

Meditation:

What are some of the major passover events of your life? For each event, identify the imminent death you faced and the new life you discovered.

Prayer:

I pray to you, LORD! Please listen. Don't hide from me in my time of trouble. Pay attention to my prayer and quickly give an answer. Future generations must also praise the LORD, so write this for them: "From his holy temple, the LORD looked down at the earth. He listened to the groans of prisoners, and he rescued everyone who was doomed to die" (Psalm 102:1-2, 18-20).

Memories:

Make a list of your relatives and friends who have already passed over through death to eternal life. Identify how each person's faith enabled him or her to pass over confidently.

Basket

Scripture:

After everyone had eaten all they wanted, Jesus' disciples picked up twelve large baskets of leftover bread and fish (Mark 6:42-43).

Reflection:

Who hasn't witnessed a basket filled with green shredded-paper grass overflowing with jelly beans, maple-flavored cream eggs, a hollow chocolate rabbit, and yellow marshmallow chicks? With a bow on its handle, the Easter basket has become a staple Easter Sunday decoration.

In the ancient world, a basket was a necessity. It was the ancient form of the paper or plastic bags we get at grocery stores today. Ancient peoples carried a basket into the marketplace and put purchased items into it for transport home. In some European countries, the daily trip to the market with a basket in hand is still a common sight.

Today, we use baskets for more decorative purposes. They may hold pine cones near a fireplace or magazines near one's favorite reading chair. In the kitchen, baskets contain onions, shallots, and garlic or tomatoes, apples, and bananas. What we can easily forget is that each of us is like an Easter basket into which God places precious gifts, which are meant to be taken out and shared with others.

Meditation:

What gifts are in your Easter basket? How do you share them with others?

Prayer:

When your people meet, you will fill my heart with your praises, LORD, and everyone will see me keep my promises to you. The poor will eat and be full, and all who worship you will be thankful and live in hope. Everyone on this earth will remember you, LORD (Psalm 22:25-27).

Memories:

Do you have an Easter basket that you bring out every year and fill with candy? Where did you get it? What do you put in it?

Chicks

Scripture:

"Would you really die for me?" Jesus asked [Peter]. "I tell you for certain that before a rooster crows, you will say three times that you don't even know me" (John 13:38).

Reflection:

A freshly-hatched chick is warm and fuzzy, and most people can't resist picking up the baby bird and cuddling it in the palm of the hand. Its incessant peep-peep reminds us that it has an insatiable hunger and a drive to sprout feathers and fly. In some places, the chick, which emerges from the tomb-like egg, represents the abundant life of resurrection.

The full-grown chick becomes a hen or rooster. And the rooster serves as a reminder of Peter's three-fold denial of Jesus—an historical fact which evangelists could not erase no matter how much they would have liked to remove that embarrassment from the church's first leader. While the story is told a little differently in each gospel, it remains there as a testimony of the fragility of faith.

The chick and Peter remind us how fragile the new life of faith really is. Both remind us how easy it is to deny a friend, to snuff out a life, to abort a fetus, to euthanize the elderly, to ignore the homeless, etc. Yes, the chick and Peter remind us that we are always in the process of coming to faith when we hear the rooster crow.

Meditation:

When you hear the rooster crow, of what fragility of life and faith does he remind you?

Prayer:

You are my God. I worship you. In my heart, I long for you, as I would long for a stream in a scorching desert. Your love means more than life to me, and I praise you. As long as I live, I will pray to you. I will sing joyful praises and be filled with excitement like a guest at a banquet (Psalm 63:1, 3-5).

Memories:

Did you ever get a new-born chick for Easter? If so, what do you remember about your pet? If not, what signs around you point to new life?

Eggs

Scripture:

Moses said to Israel: "As you walk along the road, you might see a bird's nest in a tree or on the ground. If the mother bird is in the nest with either her eggs or her baby birds, you are allowed to take the baby birds or the eggs, but not the mother bird. Let her go free, and the LORD will bless you with a long and successful life" (Deuteronomy 22:6-7).

Reflection:

Before the cholesterol conscious generation, hard-boiled eggs were standard fare with salads and lots of other dishes. Who can't remember delighting in a deviled egg? At Eastertime, children dye eggs in a rainbow of colors. Some of these are eaten, but many are hidden by adults so that youngsters can engage in an Easter egg hunt.

In the old French Missouri settlement that I came from, my ancestors talked about a custom they engaged in on Easter Sunday morning before and after Mass. They called it "egg fighting." One person would hold a hard-boiled egg in his fist with only one end barely visible. Another person would, likewise, hold an egg and fight—that is, attempt to crack the end of the opponent's egg. This process would go on and on until someone emerged from the melee with a non-cracked egg.

Today, Easter eggs come in all types and styles—from the dyed eggs children soak in food coloring to the more elaborate eggs that artists spend hours on, waxing and painting the shell. But however we use the egg, it is rich in symbolism. The Easter egg is both a tomb and a womb. Under the right conditions, out of the "womb" of the eggshell a chick emerges. And the sunrise yolk in the center of the egg white reminds us of the first rays of the sun on the first Easter Sunday morning when Jesus rose from the tomb.

Meditation:

In what ways are you like an Easter egg, a tomb and a womb for new life?

Prayer:

The LORD will bless you if you respect him and obey his laws. Your fields will produce, and you will be happy and all will go well. I pray that the LORD will bless you from Zion and let Jerusalem prosper as long as you live. May you live long enough to see your grandchildren (Psalm 128:1-2, 5-6).

In what kind of egg-dying do you engage to prepare for Easter Sunday?

Rabbit

SCRIPTURE:

[Jesus] said to the crowd, "Don't be greedy! Owning a lot of things won't make your life safe" (Luke 12:15).

REFLECTION:

No doubt you have seen a brown or white furry, long-eared, stubby-tailed burrower known as a rabbit. You may have discovered the loveable mammal gently munching grass in your front yard or enjoying the lettuce in your garden. You may have caught your foot in the rabbit's den or discovered a multitude of little naked young in your back yard.

At Eastertime the rabbit, usually referred to affectionately as a bunny, has become the equivalent of Santa Claus. He makes his appearances in malls a few weeks before Easter and poses for the camera with youngsters to whom he promises to deliver Easter baskets full of chocolate eggs on Easter Sunday.

The rabbit represents the abundance of Easter's new life because of the prolific rate at which rabbits multiply. But it also represents the fragility of abundant life. The mortality rate for both baby and adult rabbits is high. Being near the bottom of the food chain, they provide tasty meals for all types of predators. Whatever the case, it wasn't the Cadbury Bunny who delivered your dozen Easter eggs!

Meditation:

What about rabbits makes them a sign of new life for you?

Prayer:

Come, my children, listen as I teach you to respect the LORD. Do you want to live and enjoy a long life? Then don't say cruel things and don't tell lies. Do good instead of evil and try to live at peace. If you obey the LORD, he will watch over you and answer your prayers (Psalm 34:11-15).

Memories:

After spending some time in your neighborhood or in a local park and observing the rabbits you see there, make a list of what they teach you about life.

Lily

Scripture:

The LORD said, "Israel, . . . I will heal you and love you without limit. I will be like the dew— then you will blossom like lilies . . ." (Hosea 14:4-5).

Reflection:

Just like the poinsettia plant is associated with Christmas, even though it is not a winter flower, so is the lily associated with Easter, even though it is not a spring flower. The seemingly-dead bulb of the lily sends up a long green stem in summer and displays white trumpet-shaped blossoms all around the top. Of course, lilies come in a variety of colors, but it is the white Easter lily that reminds us of the resurrection.

The lily is also a sign of purity. If you look closely, you can find a pot of lilies displayed in stained glass windows depicting Mary's assumption into heaven or her coronation as queen of heaven. Likewise, in windows telling the story of Christ's resurrection, near the empty tomb there is usually a pot of lilies. The purity of the Virgin is like that of the new life of the resurrected Christ.

You too are like a lily. From deep inside you comes new life. For this new life to blossom it needs the cultivation of Lent. But after observing Lent, you trumpet new life. An Easter lily is a very appropriate sign of your purity and newness.

Meditation:

Identify times in your life when you thought you were dead only to discover that new life came forth. How were you made new?

Prayer:

The LORD is merciful! He is kind and patient, and his love never fails. We humans are like grass or wild flowers that quickly bloom. But a scorching wind blows, and they quickly wither to be forever forgotten. The LORD is always kind to those who worship him, and he keeps his promises to their descendants who faithfully obey him (Psalm 103:8, 15-18).

Memories:

What have you done with Easter lilies that you may have bought for yourself or which were given to you? If you buy or receive one this year, when it is finished blooming, plant it in your yard and record where you bury the bulb so that you can watch it grow and bloom next summer.

Lamb

Scripture:

Moses called the leaders of Israel together and said: "Each family is to pick out a sheep and kill it for Passover. Make a brush from a few small branches of a hyssop plant and dip the brush in the bowl that has the blood of the animal in it. Then brush some of the blood above the door and on the posts at each side of the door of your house" (Exodus 12:21-22).

Reflection:

The Passover ritual described above was meant to save the people of Israel from imminent death. The blood of the lamb was seen by God's angel, and all in the house, where it was smeared above and on either side of the door, were saved when he passed over with death.

Such an important scene was not lost on the author of John's Gospel. After portraying John the Baptist seeing Jesus coming toward him and saying, "Here is the Lamb of God who takes away the sin of the world!" (1:29), the evangelist proceeds to tell us that Jesus died on the eve of Passover—that would be at the same time as the lambs were being slaughtered in the temple. To be sure that we understand his reference, he adds that the soldiers did not break Jesus' legs to fulfill the Exodus prescription concerning the lamb, namely, "No bones of the Passover lamb may be broken" (Exodus 12:46; see John 19:36).

By referring to Jesus as the Passover lamb, John's Gospel declares that his blood on the wood of the cross saved him and us from eternal death. Christ's resurrection was a passover through death to life. And we who believe in him should have no fear of death, since it will only be the means of our passover from this life to eternal life.

Meditation:

What other comparisons can you make between the Passover lamb and Jesus? You can find several more examples in John's Gospel.

Prayer:

If you obey the LORD, he will watch over you and answer your prayers. When his people pray for help, he listens and rescues them from their troubles. The LORD is there to rescue all who are discouraged and have given up hope. The LORD's people may suffer a lot, but he will always bring them safely through. Not one of their bones will ever be broken (Psalm 34:15, 17-20).

What is your usual menu for Easter? Record it and update the entry every year. Have you ever served lamb, such as lamb chops, leg of lamb, or mutton?

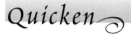

Quicken

This good news is about [God's] Son, our Lord Jesus Christ! As a human, he was from the family of David. But the Holy Spirit proved that Jesus is the powerful Son of God, because he was raised from death (Romans 1:3-4).

The verb "quicken" means "to enliven, to stimulate, to begin to show signs of life." It is often used to describe the activity of the Spirit while Jesus slept in death in the tomb. The Spirit roused Jesus to life and proved him to be God's Son, the anointed. And that was the good news Paul wrote to the Romans.

Paul understood the resurrection of Christ to be the Spirit's stimulation of the dead Jesus. He began to show signs of life, he was enlivened, three days after he was laid to rest in the tomb. On the third day there was a theophany, a manifestation of God. Quickened by the Spirit, Christ emerged filled with everlasting life.

You have been quickened by the Spirit over and over again. Through the meals you share with your family, you experience new life. Through conversations about things that really matter, you both give and receive life. Community worship, the manifestation of the church, is an act of quickening, for the Spirit enlivens all present. All these experiences of quickening are meant to help us believe that what God did for Jesus—raise him from the dead—God will do for us.

Meditation:

What has been your most recent experience of quickening? Who was involved? How was it a manifestation of God?

Prayer:

You have looked deep into my heart, LORD, and you know all about me. You are the one who put me together inside my mother's body, and I praise you because of the wonderful way you created me. Everything you do is marvelous! Of this I have no doubt (Psalm 139:1, 13-14).

Memories:

Who has been responsible for your greatest quickening? How did he or she enliven you?

Resurrection

. . . Mary . . . turned around and saw Jesus standing there. But she did not know who he was. Jesus asked her, "Why are you crying? Who are you looking for?" (John 20:14-15).

REFLECTION:

Draw a line down the middle of a page of paper. Label the line "death." Label the area to the left of death "this life," and label the area to the right of death "the next life." It's easy to fill in the "this life" side, because what we know is based on experience. But once you cross through death to the other side, what's there? We don't know. We believe that there is new or everlasting life there, but we don't know. What we attempt to describe as "waking up" or "new life" or "everlasting life" or "angels on clouds with harps" are metaphors grounded in our experiences in this life.

Presuming that he was the gardener, Mary Magdalene didn't recognize Jesus after his resurrection. We don't know what resurrection is. However, we know what it is not: It is not resuscitation or reanimation or something like a dead body getting up and walking out of a grave. Because it is on the other side of death, it will be something we have never experienced before.

The foundational belief for Christianity is that God raised Jesus from the dead. Because resurrection is transhistorical, or beyond our sense of time and place, our faith in it has no proof. We do not know what God will do after we die. We simply trust in God's faithfulness. We believe that what God did for Jesus, God will do for us.

What metaphors do you use to describe what is on the other side of death? How is each metaphor grounded in your experiences of this life?

Prayer:

You, LORD, are all I want! You are my choice, and you keep me safe. I am your chosen one. You won't leave me in the grave or let my body decay. You have shown me the path to life, and you make me glad by being near to me. Sitting at your right side, I will always be joyful (Psalm 16:5, 10-11).

Memories:

Make a list of the metaphors you have heard people use to describe resurrection. What does each simultaneously reveal and conceal about resurrection?

Moon

Scripture:

The LORD said to Moses and Aaron: "Remember this day and celebrate it each year as a festival in my honor." Moses called the leaders of Israel together and said: "After you have entered the country promised to you by the LORD, you and your children must continue to celebrate Passover each year" (Exodus 12:1, 14, 21, 24-25).

Reflection:

Passover and Easter are lunar feasts. For the Jews, Passover begins on the fourteenth day of the lunar month Nisan, which occurs during March or April. Christians also use the moon to calculate Easter. It is always the first Sunday following the first full moon after the spring equinox. Depending on the year, it is celebrated on a Sunday between March 22 and April 25.

This lunar method for determining Easter was set by the Council of Nicaea in 325 in order to set a definite way of both calculating and determining the day for the feast. Since the date of Christmas too was originally determined by the winter solstice, an ancient feast in honor of the *sol invictus* (nonconquered sun) transformed by early Christians into the nonconquered Son of God, it was only appropriate that the moon be used to calculate Easter. Because of primitive means of calculation, the date for Easter couldn't be determined until early in the year. So, on the Solemnity of Epiphany the dates for Ash Wednesday and Easter were announced.

Until the seventeenth century, astrologers presumed that the earth was the center of the universe. Every night the moon waxed and waned across the sky, sometimes bright, sometimes barely noticeable, sometimes a slim crescent. And it took about 28 (27 1/3 to be exact) days for it to complete what came to be called its phases. Now we know that the moon is a satellite of the earth, even though people of the past attributed divine power to it and believed it to be a goddess who ruled the night. The second day of the week is named after the moon—Moon-day.

In what other ways does the moon affect you?

Prayer:

Be happy and shout to God who makes us strong! Shout praises to the God of Jacob. Sing as you play tambourines and the lovely sounding stringed instruments. Sound the trumpets and start the New Moon Festival. We must also celebrate when the moon is full (Psalm 81:1-3).

Memories:

Find out when Passover will be celebrated. Compose a prayer for God's chosen people and pray it during their eight-day observance of their liberation from Egyptian slavery.

Night

Scripture:

The LORD said to Moses and Aaron: "That same night I will pass through Egypt and kill the first-born son in every family and the first-born male of all animals. I am the LORD, and I will punish the gods of Egypt. The blood on the houses will show me where you live, and when I see the blood, I will pass over you. Then you won't be bothered by the terrible disasters I will bring on Egypt" (Exodus 12:1, 12-13).

Reflection:

The first Passover took place at night. After slaughtering a lamb, the Hebrews took some of its blood and daubed it above their doors and on their doorposts. Then, after roasting its flesh, they ate it fully dressed with sandals on their feet and a staff in hand. And they awaited God's passing over them.

Because the first Passover took place during the night, the Easter Vigil is held during the night. Once the fire is kindled and the Easter Candle is lit and carried solemnly in procession into the darkened church, a minister sings the Easter proclamation. During that ancient hymn, we hear the phrase "this is the night" repeated. This is the night when God first saved the Hebrews. This is the night when the pillar of fire kept pharaoh's army from God's people. This night is truly blessed because God has wedded heaven to earth. This is the night of baptism. This is the night when Christ rose from the grave.

Most people think of darkness as evil, but it is holy. Under the cover of darkness, the holy flashes out. A darkened church is conducive to prayer. Conversations between friends or lovers come from the depths of people sitting in the dark. We can see each other more clearly in the darkness. Many people pass over through death to life during the night.

Meditation:

What recent special event of your life has occurred during the night? How was God present? What light flashed from the holy?

Our God and King, you have ruled since ancient times; you have won victories everywhere on this earth. You rule the day and the night, and you put the moon and the sun in place. You made summer and winter and gave them to the earth (Psalm 74:12, 16-17).

Memories:

Make a list of the transforming events of your life, like graduation, marriage, birth of a child, etc. Indicate which of these events took place during the night.

(Good) Shepherd

Scripture:

Jesus said, "I am the good shepherd, and the good shepherd gives up his life for his sheep" (John 10:11).

Reflection:

Every year on the Fourth Sunday of Easter, we hear a selection from the narrative in John's Gospel about Jesus being a good shepherd. Most people do not realize how ironic the phrase "good shepherd" is. In popular understanding, there was no such person as a good shepherd, like there was no good Samaritan.

Shepherds were considered outcasts in the ancient world. They were robbers, who stole food wherever they could find it. They pastured their sheep on other people's land until they were driven off. Often dirty because they lived outdoors on the land, they didn't observe Jewish purity codes. Thus, they were unclean.

So, when Jesus declares himself to be the good shepherd, he associates himself with society's outcasts. He declares himself to be one who looks after others on the fringes of the community. If they are ritually impure, this makes him the most unclean of all. And such a designation enables him to shepherd all of humanity.

Meditation:

How is Jesus your good shepherd?

Prayer:

You, LORD, are my shepherd. I will never be in need. You let me rest in fields of green grass. You lead me to streams of peaceful water, and you refresh my life (Psalm 23:1-3).

Memories:

Since shepherds and sheep are usually removed from our experience, how would you describe Jesus' role of leading and guiding you today?

Trumpet

Once every forty-nine years on the tenth day of the seventh month, which is also the Great Day of Forgiveness, trumpets are to be blown everywhere in the land. This fiftieth year is sacred—it is a time of freedom and of celebration . . . (Leviticus 25:8-10).

Reflection:

In biblical literature the blowing of a trumpet signals that God is speaking. Every fiftieth year, the Israelites were instructed to celebrate a year of freedom which began with a trumpet blast to indicate both that it was a gift from God and that it was required by God.

From Ash Wednesday's trumpet blown to proclaim a fast to the last trumpet blast on Pentecost Sunday, God speaks to us intently. Indeed, if we listen carefully, God blows a trumpet every day. God's call to cooperate with the divine plan comes to us in many ways: through the members of our family, through our coworkers, through the books we read, and through the Bible.

When we listen to God's trumpet blast and cooperate with God, we are set free. It is not a freedom to do as we wish, but to do as required. The freedom God offers is one that flows from our innermost being because it liberates us to be who God calls us to be. And if that isn't worth blowing a trumpet, then what is?

What recent trumpet have you heard God blow? How did you cooperate with God? What freedom did you experience?

Prayer:

Everyone on this earth will remember you, LORD. People all over the world will turn and worship you, because you are in control, the ruler of all nations. All who are rich and have more than enough will bow down to you, Lord. Even those who are dying and almost in the grave will come and bow down. In the future, everyone will worship and learn about you, our Lord. People not yet born will be told, "The Lord has saved us!" (Psalm 22:27-31).

Memories:

Make a list of as many trumpet blasts as you can remember from your life. For each remembrance, identify what freedom you experienced and how each was a summons to cooperate with God.

Unity

Scripture:

The Spirit has given each of us a special way of serving others. The body of Christ has many different parts, just as any other body does. But

God's Spirit baptized each of us and made us part of the body of Christ. Now we each drink from that same Spirit (1 Corinthians 12:7, 12-13).

Reflection:

We have a strong tendency to categorize people according to religious affiliation. So, when we hear the names of world religions, like Judaism, Christianity, Islam, Buddhism, Hinduism, Taoism, etc., we put specific people into each of those categories, which means that when we include them in one category, we automatically exclude them from another.

As in other world religions, within Christianity there are many denominations, groups of Christians, sometimes referred to as churches. From the perspective of a church, people easily fall into the practice of presuming that they belong to the right Christian church and all others are wrong. If we would only look at this from a universal point of view, we'd see that if every church excludes all others, then all are excluded.

That's not how Paul saw the church when he wrote to the Corinthians. He looked at its unity. He saw it as the one body of Christ with many different members, each having a function of service within and to the whole. Beginning with its inclusivity, Paul saw the church not as a community formed by its members, but as the body created by the Spirit, the source of their unity. Thus, all were included and no one excluded.

Meditation:

What works of unity do you find among Christians where you live? How are these works of service inspired by the Spirit?

Everyone who serves the LORD, come and offer praises. Everyone who has gathered in his temple tonight, lift your hands in prayer toward his holy place and praise the LORD. The LORD is the Creator of heaven and earth, and I pray that the LORD will bless you from Zion (Psalm 134:1-3).

MEMORIES:

What have been some of your experiences of exclusivity and inclusivity? What does each teach you about the importance of unity?

Yeast

SCRIPTURE:

Stop being proud! Don't you know how a little yeast can spread through the whole batch of dough? Get rid of the old yeast! Then you will be like fresh bread made without yeast, and that is what you are. Our Passover lamb is Christ, who has already been sacrificed (1 Corinthians 5:6-7).

REFLECTION:

When preparing to make bread, we know that we need yeast. So we go to the baking department of the grocery store and purchase a packet of yeast. After activating it in warm water, we mix it into the dough and watch it rise. With our scientific understanding, we know that it's the reproduction and multiplication of the single-cell fungi that make the bread rise.

However, in the ancient world yeast or leaven was synonymous with corruption. People in the first century common era didn't understand how yeast worked. So, they labeled it corrupt. Thus, for special days in honor of God, like Passover, only unleavened bread could be made and eaten. Corruption could not be used to worship God. That's why Paul tells the Corinthians to get rid of the corruption of pride. It spreads throughout the community, like yeast in dough, corrupting all whom it touches.

Then, Paul associates Christ with the Passover lamb. Until the destruction of Jerusalem in 70 C.E. by the Romans, the Jews marked Passover by sacrificing a lamb in the Temple. Its blood was poured on the altar, but its flesh was eaten by the members of every family who prepared it. Paul declares that there is a new Passover lamb, Jesus Christ, who, being without blemish or pride, shows us how to live noncorrupting lives.

Meditation:

What corrupts you? Think in terms of the technological world you live in, the Internet, stock investments, pornography, consumerism, etc.

Prayer:

I am God Most High! The only sacrifice I want is for you to be thankful and to keep your word. Pray to me in time of trouble. I will rescue you, and you will honor me. The sacrifice that honors me is a thankful heart. Obey me, and I, your God, will show my power to save (Psalm 50:14-15, 23).

If you make and bake bread, what does that task teach you about your relationship with God? If you don't make or bake bread, how do you corrupt others with God?

Cristos (Christ)

SCRIPTURE:

The first thing Andrew did was to find his brother and tell him, "We have found the Messiah!" The Hebrew word "Messiah" means the same as the Greek word "Christ" (John 1:41).

REFLECTION:

Jesus' last name is not Christ, as some children think. "Christ" (in Greek "Cristos") means "anointed," just like the Hebrew "Messiah" does. In Greek, "chi" represents the "Ch" of English. As the author of John's Gospel explains, finding the Messiah is also finding the Christ, God's anointed.

Jesus was called the Christ by biblical authors to tie him into the royal line of David, which had come to an end in 587 B.C.E. with the Babylonian capture of Jerusalem, the exile of its citizens, and the eventual death of Israel's last king, Zedekiah. By referring to Jesus as Christ, the authors of the New Testament declare that God has begun a new royal line.

After baptism, you were anointed with chrism (Christ) oil. During the Easter Vigil, after catechumens are baptized, they are anointed with this sweet-smelling oil. Confirmed and strengthened in their faith, they are told to live it as other Christs—as members of his priestly, prophetic, royal people. In other words, just like you, the newly-baptized are declared to be members of God's new royals.

Meditation:

What does it mean to you to be a member of God's royal family?

Prayer:

You are God, and you will rule forever as king. Your royal power brings about justice. You love justice and hate evil. And so, your God chose you and made you happier than any of your friends. The sweet aroma of the spices myrrh, aloes, and cassia, covers your royal robes (Psalm 45:6-8).

Memories:

What sweet-smelling oil do you use? How can it remind you that you are one of God's royal, chosen people?

Ascension

For forty days after Jesus had suffered and died, he proved in many ways that he had been raised from death. He appeared to his apostles and spoke to them about God's kingdom. . . . While they were watching, he was taken up into a cloud. They could not see him, but as he went up, they kept looking up into the sky (Acts 1:3, 9-10).

REFLECTION:

In some countries, Ascension is celebrated forty days after Easter Sunday on Thursday, while in others it is celebrated on the Seventh Sunday of Easter. What most people find interesting is that in Luke's Gospel the Ascension occurs on Easter Sunday after several of Jesus' post-resurrection appearances to his disciples. According to Luke, the author of both the gospel and the Acts of the Apostles, as Jesus was blessing his disciples, "he left and was taken up to heaven" (Luke 24:51).

Why would the author portray Jesus' ascension once on Easter Sunday and once forty days later? Because he did not understand Ascension as an historical event. Thinking theologically, he viewed ascension as resurrection. Once he portrayed Jesus making post-resurrection appearances, he had to get him "out of the picture" in order to write about the missionary activity of the disciples. If Jesus were still present, there would be no need for the disciples to begin spreading the news that God had raised him from the dead.

For us, ascension represents vision. As each of us makes his or her pilgrimage through life, we need a vision of where we are going. This is true of our financial, environmental, physical, emotional, and spiritual lives. If our sights are set on God's reign, we will discover that we are engaged in spreading the word, and we can expect that one day God will raise us or we will ascend to God, like Jesus did.

Meditation:

What is your vision of a Christian life?

Prayer:

All of you nations, clap your hands and shout joyful praises to God. God goes up to his throne, as people shout and trumpets blast. Sing praises to God our King, the ruler of all the earth! Praise God with songs (Psalm 47:1, 5-7).

Memories:

Make a list of things that go up, like spacecraft, balloons, airplanes. Identify how each can help you expand your vision of a Christian lifestyle.

Pentecost (Sunday)

SCRIPTURE:

On the day of Pentecost all the Lord's followers were together in one place. Suddenly there was a noise from heaven like the sound of a mighty wind! It filled the house where they were meeting. Then they saw what looked like fiery tongues moving in all directions, and a tongue came and settled on each person there. The Holy Spirit took control of everyone, and they began speaking whatever languages the Spirit let them speak (Acts 2:1-4).

REFLECTION:

Occurring fifty days after Easter and bringing the Easter Season to a close, Pentecost Sunday focuses on the manifestation of the Spirit and the Spirit's connection to our spirit. In other words, Pentecost is about our lifeline to God.

Using a variety of metaphors, the author of the Acts of the Apostles attempts to capture in words the truth that our spirit is enlivened by God's Spirit. Fire signifies God's presence throughout the scriptures. Wind, blowing before creation began, brings order out of chaos. The breath of life, the spirit, blown into the first people God made from clay, becomes a mighty wind filling us with the Spirit.

When God's Spirit mingles with our spirits, God's presence flames out in our lives. When spirit touches spirit, relationships are born and friends exchange the Spirit with each other. The silence between the words of preachers becomes a new language communicating the

Spirit. And every breath we take not only keeps us alive, but inspires our spirit with Spirit.

Meditation:

In what ways have you experienced God's Spirit?

Prayer:

Our LORD, by your wisdom you made so many things; the whole earth is covered with your living creatures. All of these depend on you to provide them with food, and you feed each one with your own hand, until they are full. You created all of them by your Spirit, and you give new life to the earth (Psalm 104:24, 27-28, 30).

Memories:

What is your most memorable celebration of Pentecost? What made it so?

Blessings
for
Lent
and
Easter

Blessing of Ashes

Leader: Blessed are you, Lord our God, who created us from the dust of the earth and breathed the breath of life into us. May these ashes remind us of our mortality and your gift of eternal life. Make our repentance be genuine and draw us closer to you. You are God for ever and ever.

All: Amen.

Blessing of a Cross

Leader: Blessed are you, Lord our God, who displayed Jesus on the cross. Let this cross remind us of his loving gift of obedience to you and his victory over death. Help us to carry our daily crosses as we observe this season of grace. Strengthen us now and forever.

All: Amen.

Blessing of a Candle

Leader: Blessed are you, Lord our God, who gives us the light of the sun during the day and the moon during the night. Bless this candle, which represents Jesus Christ, the light of the world. May its light always draw us closer to you so that we glow with your light of grace. Praise to you now and for ever and ever.

All: Amen.

Blessing of the Home

Leader: Blessed are you, Lord our God, creator of the earth and of all who live on the third planet from the sun. Come and make your dwelling place in this temple. May our observance of Lent and Easter draw us closer together in your presence. Let our praise and thanks rise from our home to your home in heaven, for ever and ever.

All: Amen.

Blessing of Palm Branches

Leader: Blessed are you, Lord our God, who gives us these palm branches to recall the triumphal entry of your Son, Jesus, into Jerusalem. May his victory over death give us courage to face our daily dying and rising. May all praise and glory be yours now and for ever.

All: Hosanna in the highest!

Blessing of Water

(All gather around a small bowl of water.)

Leader: Blessed are you, Lord our God, maker of all springs, rivers, seas, and oceans. May this water be a sign of our baptism and the new life of grace we share with you. Draw us closer to you and make our lives living springs gushing with everlasting life. All glory be yours now and for ever.

All: Amen.

Renewal of Baptismal Promises

Leader: Do you reject sin and refuse to be mastered by sin so as to live in the freedom of God's children?

All: I do.

Leader: Do you believe in God, the Father almighty, creator of heaven and earth; in Jesus Christ, his only Son, our Lord, who was born of the Virgin Mary, was crucified, died, and was buried, rose from the dead, and is now seated at the right hand of the Father; and in the Holy Spirit, the holy catholic church, the communion of saints, the forgiveness of sins, the resurrection of the body, and life everlasting?

All: I do.

Leader: God has given us new birth through water and the Holy Spirit. May God keep us faithful to our baptismal promises for ever and ever.

All: Amen.

(Each person, after dipping a hand in the water, makes the sign of the cross with the water.)

Blessing of Food on Ash Wednesday

Leader: Blessed are you, Lord our God, who gives us this season of forty days to fast, to give alms, and to pray. Through our observance of Lent, bring about conversion in our lives. May our sharing of this food make us pleasing in your sight. All praise to you now and for ever.

All: Amen.

Blessing of Food
During the First Week of Lent

Leader: Blessed are you, Lord our God, creator of the earth and all it produces. Through our fasting from your gifts, make us appreciate and desire them more. May our simple meal fill us with a deeper hunger for you. May our sharing give you praise for ever and ever.

All: Amen.

Blessing of Food
During the Second Week of Lent

Leader: Blessed are you, Lord our God, who transforms everything by your spoken word. May our Lenten prayer, the words that come from our mouths, be pleasing in your sight. May we listen with attentive ears in the same way as we eat with joyful hearts. Praise to you now and for ever.

All: Amen.

Blessing of Food
During the Third Week of Lent

Leader: Blessed are you, Lord our God, who calls people to serve each other. Guide our footsteps throughout our Lenten journey to all who are in need, especially those who hunger for justice. May our almsgiving of time, talent, and treasure bring us into deeper communion with them and you. We give you praise now and for ever.

All: Amen.

Blessing of Food
During the Fourth Week of Lent

Leader: Blessed are you, Lord our God, who washes away our blindness and brings us home. Open our eyes to see those who hunger and thirst. Give us repentant hearts so that our Lenten journey leads us home to you. May this food you bless give us the strength to praise you for ever.

All: Amen.

Blessing of Food
During the Fifth Week of Lent

Leader: Blessed are you, Lord our God, who from death brings life, who from despair brings hope, who from hunger brings fullness. Strengthen us with this food, a gift from your hands. Through our union with Christ, transform our dying into new life. All glory be yours now and for ever and ever.

All: Amen.

Blessing of Food
During Holy Week

Leader: Blessed are you, Lord our God, who gives us days and weeks to live in your presence. As we remember the great events that brought us new life in Jesus Christ, bless this food and our sharing of it. May we never forget that from your hand comes all good gifts. Praise be to you for ever and ever.

All: Hosanna in the highest!

Blessing of Food
During the Easter Triduum

Leader: Blessed are you, Lord our God, who teaches us to wash each other's feet in service, who shows us how to do your will through the cross, who displays for us the transforming power of the resurrection. As we serve each other, help us to carry our cross with the hope of sharing new life with you. Strengthen us through this food we share. Praise to you for ever and ever.

All: Amen.

Blessing of Food
on Easter Sunday

Leader: Alleluia! Blessed are you, Lord our God, who made your Son, Jesus Christ, our paschal sacrifice. He is our passover lamb, who gives us the food and drink of everlasting life. May this food and drink remind us of his eucharistic gift of bread and wine, his body and blood, and strengthen us to serve you all our days. Alleluia! Alleluia!

All: Alleluia! Alleluia!

Blessing of Food
During the First Week of Easter

Leader: Alleluia! Blessed are you, Lord our God, who awakened Jesus Christ from the sleep of death to the new life and light of the resurrection. May this food bring us health of mind and body. Alleluia!

All: Alleluia!

Blessing of Food
During the Second Week of Easter

Leader: Alleluia! Blessed are you, Lord our God, who gives faith in the resurrection of your Son, Jesus Christ, to those who doubt. With this food strengthen our bodies and our faith in your power to raise the dead. Remove our doubts and fill us with new life. Alleluia!

All: Alleluia!

Blessing of Food
During the Third Week of Easter

Leader: Alleluia! Blessed are you, Lord our God, who revealed your Son, Jesus Christ, in the breaking of bread. May the bread we share be a sign of our unity as members of the body of Christ. May its breaking be a sign of our willingness to serve each other. Alleluia!

All: Alleluia!

Blessing of Food
During the Fourth Week of Easter

Leader: Alleluia! Blessed are you, Lord our God, the Shepherd who never leaves us unattended. You lead us to the pastures of your grace. You anoint our heads with your healing touch. You give us food to nourish our lives and spirits. May our sharing of this food give you praise. Alleluia!

All: Alleluia!

Blessing of Food
During the Fifth Week of Easter

Leader: Alleluia! Blessed are you, Lord our God, who draws us together to share your life, like branches on the vine. May this food make us aware of the growth of your life within us. May our celebration of Easter give you glory. Alleluia!

All: Alleluia!

Blessing of Food
During the Sixth Week of Easter

Leader: Alleluia! Blessed are you, Lord our God, for you overwhelm us with the gift of your Spirit. Open our minds and our hearts to be ready to receive your gift. Bless the food we share so that it will make us obedient to your word. Alleluia!

All: Alleluia!

Blessing of Food
on Ascension

Leader: Alleluia! Blessed are you, Lord our God, who is present with us throughout our lives. Through the ascension of your Son, Jesus Christ, make us joyful. Through our sharing of this food, make us aware of your presence with us until the end of time. Alleluia!

All: Alleluia!

Blessing of Food
on the Seventh Sunday of Easter

Leader: Alleluia! Blessed are you, Lord our God, who are three persons and one God. May the unity you share as Father, Son, and Spirit be the desire of our family. Make this sharing of food a sign of our unity with each other and with you. Alleluia!

All: Alleluia!

Blessing of Food
on Pentecost Sunday

Leader: Blessed are you, Lord our God, who with a mighty wind and fire and language sent on mission the disciples of your Son. Make us thirsty for the living water of Jesus Christ. Strengthen us with this food so that we can tell of the great things you have done. Alleluia! Alleluia!

All: Alleluia! Alleluia!

FR. MARK G. BOYER is the editor of *The Mirror*, the diocesan newspaper for Springfield-Cape Girardeau, Missouri. He is the author of twenty-two books and many articles on spirituality, prayer, and the seasons of the church year. His ministry of more than twenty-five years has included teaching, writing, editing, and parish work.